Alba Workbook for Books

CW01668260

Contents

The Phonic Code

Consonant Sound Spellings

'j'
j jet
g (eiy) gentle
ge barge
dge judge

'n'
n no
nn planning
kn know
gn gnat
pn pneumonia

'z'
z zip
zz buzz
s is
se choose
ze snooze
x xylophone

'h'
h hot
wh whole

'l'
l lip
ll full
le apple
el travel
il pupil
al final

'g'
g rag
gg juggle
gh ghost

'd'
d did
ed grabbed
dd muddle

'zh'
s leisure
ge prestige
z seizure

'k'
k kite
c cat
ck duck
ch Christmas
que antique
q Iraq

'm'
m man
mm summer
mb lamb
mn Autumn

'y'
y yes

'sh'
sh shop
ch machine
s sugar

's'
s sip
ss grass
c (eiy) cent
ce voice
se house
st castle
sc science
ps psychic

't'
t tin
tt getting
bt debt
pt pterodactyl
te granite

'ks'
'x'
x fox
cc accept

'r'
r rat
wr write
rr carry
rh rhino

'v'
v very
ve have

'ch'
ch chip
tch match

'w'
w wig
wh when

'gz'
'x'
x exam

'qu'
qu queen

'p'
p hop
pp happy

'f'
f fat
ff staff
ph phone
gh laugh
ffe giraffe

'b'
b big
bb rabbit

'th'
th moth
th that (voiced)

Vowel Sound Spellings

'oe'
o most
o-e note
oe toe
oa boat
ow grow
ough though
ou soul
ew sew

'a'
a cat

'o'
o not
a was

'ie'
i wild
ie pie
i-e like
igh night
y dry
eigh height

'ee'
e me
ee meet
ea seat
e-e eve
ie chief
y funny
ey key
ei re(c) eive
i variation
eo people

'ae'
a table
ai rain
a-e game
ea great
ay say
ey they
ei vein
aigh straight
eigh eight

'aw'
au fraud
aw lawn
a ball
al walk
or for
our your
ore more
oor door
oar board
(w)ar warm
ough fought
augh daughter

'e'
e bed
ea bread
ai said
ie friend
eo leopard

'er'
er perk
ur turn
ir girl
or world
ear learn
our colour
ar collar
re centre
yr zephyr

'oo'
oo cook
oul could
u put
o woman

'i'
i in
y myth

'u'
u tub
ou touch
o-e some
a about
o Monday
oo blood

'ar'
a glass
al calm
ar jar
er clerk
ear heart

'ow'
ow cow
ou out
ough drought

'oi'
oi join
oy boy

'ue'
u-e mule
u pupil
ew few
ue cue

'air'
air chair
are dare
ear bear
eir their
ere where
ayor mayor
ayer prayer
ae aeroplane

'oo'
oo boot
ue blue
ew grew
u super
ui suit
u-e flute
ou soup
oe shoe
o do
ough through

www.phonicbooks.co.uk

Notes on the Alba Series

Introduction

The Alba Series is aimed at older pupils who would benefit from going back to the very beginning of learning the Phonic Code. This series is designed as a parallel series to the Totem Series in terms of phonic structure and sequence. It begins with cvc and cvcc words and includes consonant digraphs and some of the alternative vowel spellings.

The Alba Series comprises twelve books. A comprehensive workbook based on the stories includes a variety of activities which teach and consolidate an understanding of the Phonic Code.

Order of the books

The books in the series have a step-by-step progression and should, therefore, be read in the numbered sequence.

Pace of teaching

The Alba Series and workbook is an accelerated catch-up reading programme. It should be taught at a pace suited to the pupil. Some books include a number of phonemes or graphemes. It is important that, at each stage, the reader is taught the phonemes and graphemes **before** reading the books. This will ensure success and the building of confidence at each level. The word level activities in the early parts of each chapter of the workbook are designed to help with this. These activities should preferably be done before reading the book.

Pronunciation

Pronunciation of some sounds may vary, according to regional accents. The word lists may not always match the pronunciation of the pupil. This point should be discussed and the lists adapted to the pupil.

Blending not guessing

Pupils should be encouraged to blend the sounds into words. If there are spellings they do not know, point to the part of the word that is new and tell them the sound. Then get the pupil to blend the sounds into the word.

Use precise pronunciation

When blending sounds together, say the consonants without the added 'uh' sound,
e.g. 'c' 'a' 't' not 'cuh' 'a' 'tuh'.

Teaching alternative spellings

The English Phonic Code is complex. This series presents a number of alternative spellings for a vowel sound. The teacher may need to introduce these spellings gradually if the pupil has difficulty learning all the alternative spellings at a time.

Splitting multisyllabic words

At the bottom of every page in the books, a few multisyllabic words are split for the reader. This will enable the reader to tackle longer words independently.
There are a number of ways to split multisyllabic words.
The approach taken in this series is to split the word in the most 'reader-friendly' way.

New vocabulary

Each new book offers an opportunity to learn new vocabulary on the vocabulary page. This page explains the words as they appear in the context of the text. The teacher may wish to discuss additional meanings of the word with the pupil.

Reading practice

A reading practice page is included at the beginning of each book. From Book 6, these pages contain alternative spellings of the vowel sounds in the book. These pages can be very useful for preparing pupils for the phonic focus of the text.

Notes on the Alba Workbook

This workbook complements the Alba Series. Twelve chapters in the workbook correlate to the twelve books in the series. Each chapter offers activities based on the phonic focus of each of the books. Before reading the books, pupils would benefit from practising word-building, blending, reading and sorting activities. These activities feature at the beginning of every chapter. Follow-up activities, such as comprehension, spelling and writing, should be introduced after reading the texts. The teacher can select from the activities in each chapter to maintain interest and variety.

All activities are fully photocopiable.

An instruction for every activity in the workbook appears at the bottom of each page.

The split vowel spellings can be particularly tricky for pupils to master. With this in mind, chapters 6, 8 and 11 of the workbook (which include split vowel spellings) have been designed to include additional activities to help support the learning of the reading and spelling of these.

N.B. Exercises which ask the pupil to identify real words may not be suitable for pupils with a poor vocabulary. The teacher can introduce them as blending exercises.

Phonic Sequence in the Alba Series: Books 1 to 12

Book	Title	Phoneme focus	Spelling
1	Lost	cvc, cvcc	cvc and cvcc words
2	The Plan	ccvc	ccvc words
3	Alba Slips Up	ccvcc	ccvcc words
4	Hot Chips for Lunch	'sh' 'ch' 'th'	sh ch tch th
5	A Bit of Luck	'ck' 'ng' 'qu' 'wh' 'le' –ed	ck ng qu wh le –ed
6	A Brave Escape	'ae'	ay ai a a–e
7	Apple Trees	'ee'	ee ea y ey e
8	The Long Road Home	'oe'	o ow oa o–e
9	Supper	'er'	er ir ur
10	Howling Wind	'ow'	ow ou
11	River Flight	'ie'	igh y ie i–e
12	The Truth	'oo'	oo u u–e ew

Alba Series Workbook for Books 1 – 12

This book belongs to

....

Pupils can use this page as a personalised front cover for their Alba Series work.

Alba Series pupil reading record

name :

Book 1

Book 2

Book 3

Book 4

Book 5

Book 6

Book 7

Book 8

Book 9

Book 10

Book 11

Book 12

This sheet can be used by either pupil or teacher as a means of recording progression through the series. Boxes can be ticked or dated as required.

Book 1: Lost

Phonic focus: cvc and cvcc **Spellings:** cvc and cvcc words

Contents

Book 1: Word–building cvc words

c	a	t
c	*a*	*t*

Teaching aims:

- Segment and blend cvc (consonant/vowel/consonant) words with the sounds of the alphabet.

Teaching guidelines:
Use a white board on which three lines have been drawn. Use the cards from the appendix for word–building.

Teach word–building:
Select a word from the list below. Use only the letters needed to build that word and jumble them up. Ask the pupil to build that word by listening to the sounds in the words and segmenting all the sounds in the words, one at a time. The pupil then brings down each card once he/she has segmented the sound in the word. Ask the pupil to read the word he/she has built. Ask the pupil to write the word under the lines, saying the sounds as he/she writes each sound.

Word list for word–building, reading and spelling:
map, run, yap, vet, kit, can, but, hot, leg, fin, bag, sun, zip, rod, jet, wig, box

Book 1: Reading and spelling cvc words

cap	✓	___ ___ ___	
pen		___ ___ ___	
win		___ ___ ___	
jog		___ ___ ___	
sun		___ ___ ___	
fat		___ ___ ___	
red		___ ___ ___	
zip		___ ___ ___	
hot		___ ___ ___	

Teaching aims: Reading and spelling cvc words

Teaching guidelines: Trim off this text box and fold the sheet along the dotted line. Ask the pupil to read the words on the left and tick the words she/he has read correctly. Ask the pupil to turn over the sheet. Dictate the words one at a time, encouraging the pupil to spell the words by segmenting and sounding out the sounds as she/he writes them. The pupil can then open the sheet and tick the words she/he has spelled correctly.

Words for dictation: cap pen win jog sun fat red zip hot

Book 1: Reading accuracy cvc words

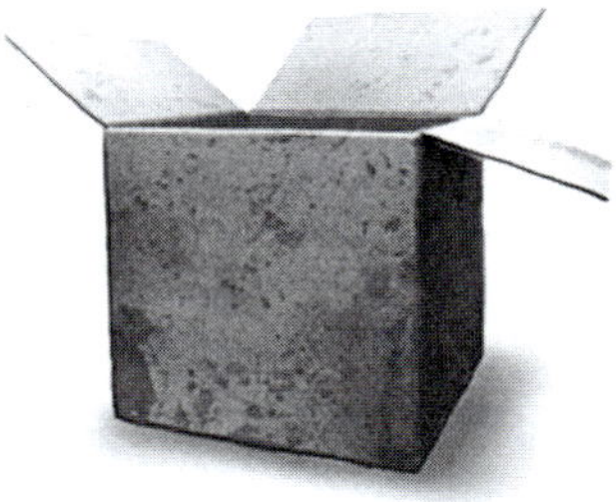

fox
bad
box

sip
sad
sat

zip
zap
fez

pat
tap
pin

cub
cup
cut

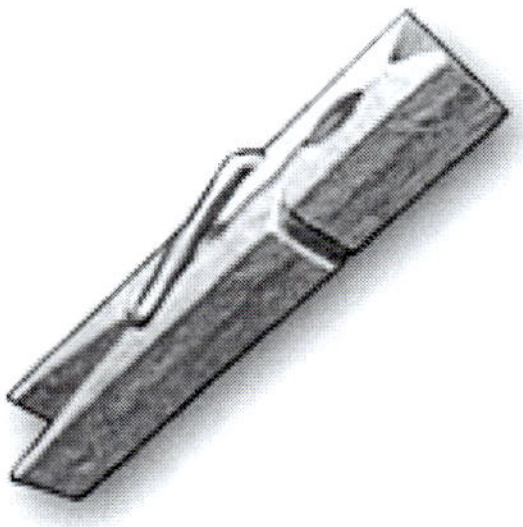

pig
pen
peg

Teaching aim: Reading accuracy

Teaching guidelines: Ask the pupil to read the words in each box and circle the word that matches the picture.

Book 1: Medial vowels (cvc): Is it a real word?

a	e	i	o	u
b a d ✔	b e d ✔	b i d ✔	b o d X	b u d ✔
h _ m	h _ m	h _ m	h _ m	h _ m

a	e	i	o	u
b _ n	b _ n	b _ n	b _ n	b _ n
r _ g	r _ g	r _ g	r _ g	r _ g

a	e	i	o	u
t _ b	t _ b	t _ b	t _ b	t _ b
v _ t	v _ t	v _ t	v _ t	v _ t

Teaching aim: Reading accuracy

Teaching guidelines: Cut this sheet into three horizontal strips. Ask the pupil to insert the vowel sound into the space in each word and blend the sounds to read the word. Put a tick next to a real word and a cross next to a nonsense word.

Book 1: Reading practice cvc words

mat	vet	sit
win	get	fun
bed	bad	lot
gut	not	cap
fit	hat	kit
rot	yet	jam
tax	zip	cvc words (Alba Book 1)

Teaching aim: Reading practice

Teaching guidelines: Photocopy this page onto card and cut into reading cards

Book 1: Reading and spelling
Two-syllable words (cvc level)

lap/top	✓	__ __ __/__ __ __	
bed/bug		__ __ __/__ __ __	
Bat/man		__ __ __/__ __ __	
cat/nap		__ __ __/__ __ __	
ad/mit		__ __/__ __ __	
ban/dit		__ __ __/__ __ __	
ex/it		__ __/__ __	
kid/nap		__ __ __/__ __ __	
cab/in		__ __ __/__ __	

Teaching aims: Reading and spelling words with cvc syllables

Teaching guidelines: Fold this sheet along the dotted line. Ask the pupil to read the words on the left and tick the words she/he has read correctly. Ask the pupil to turn over the sheet and dictate the words to the pupil. Ask the pupil to spell the words by segmenting and sounding out the sounds as she/he writes them on the lines. Ask the pupil to open the sheet and tick the words she/he has spelled correctly.

Book 1: Reading practice
Two-syllable words (cvc level)

nutmeg	wigwam	cosmic
edit	cabin	fossil
magnet	comic	bandit
atlas	cobweb	hatbox
catnap	laptop	picnic
convex	candid	rabbit
kidnap	bedbug	Two-syllable words cvc level (Alba Book 1)

Teaching aim: Reading practice

Teaching guidelines: Photocopy this page onto card and cut into reading cards

Book 1: 4–in–a–row game (cvc)

cat	bed	fun	hit	mug
pet	pat	fin	wok	run
tip	zip	vet	dog	mat
hut	lap	jam	sun	red
yet	bat	fox	lot	run
bet	sad	bin	mud	mop
man	peg	jug	jog	kit

A game for two players: Play with two sets of coloured counters. Players take turns to read a word and put a counter on it. The winner is the first to get four of his or her counters in a row in any direction. The winner places a counter on an apple symbol. The game is played four times until all the apple symbols are covered.

Book 1: Stepping stones reading game (cvc) words

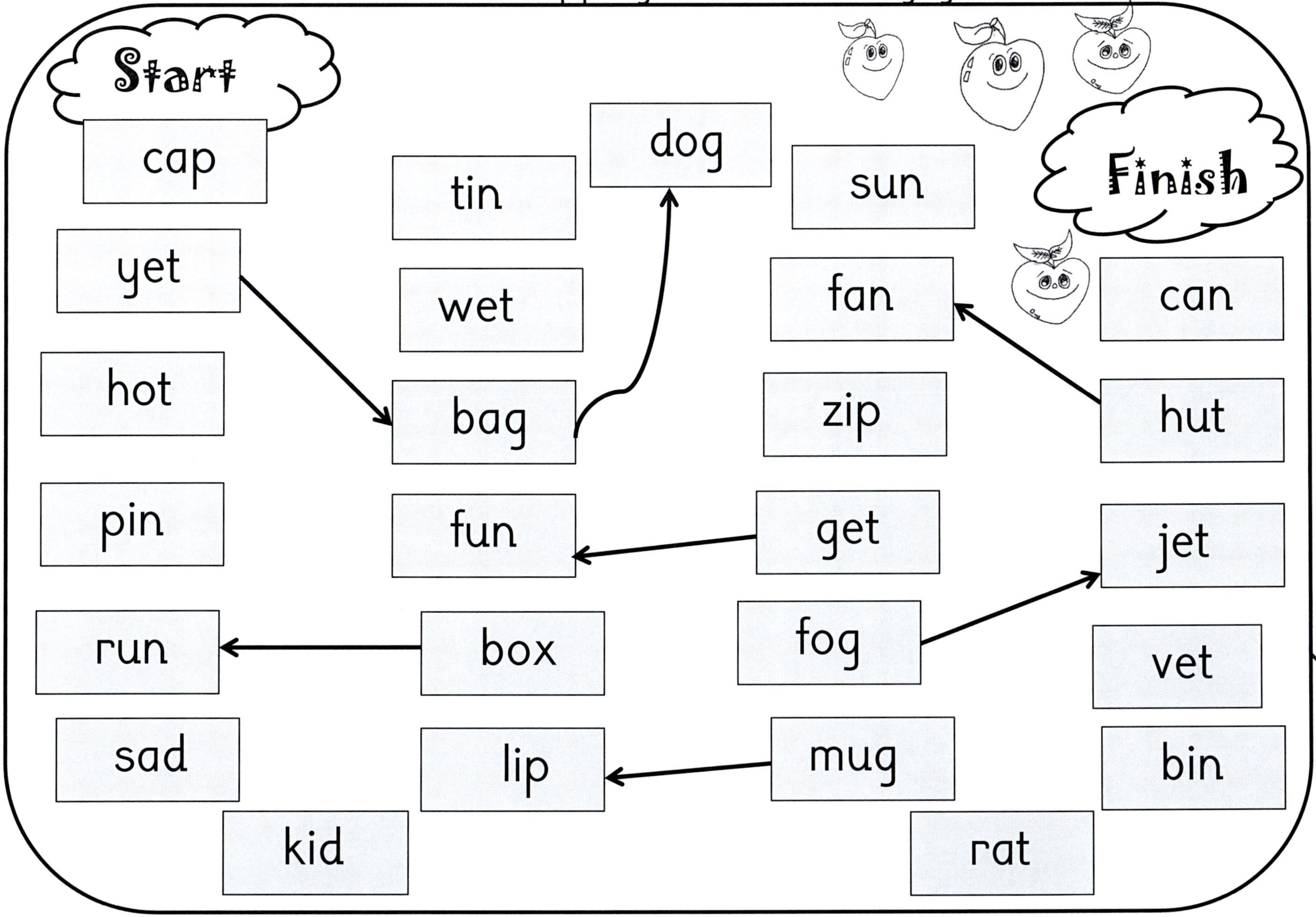

A game for 1–4 players: Play with counters and dice. Players should read aloud the words that they land on at the end of each turn and follow the direction arrows if they land on them.

Book 1: Word-building cvcc words

l	o	s	t
l	*o*	*s*	*t*

Teaching aims:

- Segment and blend cvcc (consonant/vowel/consonant/consonant) words with the sounds of the alphabet.

Teaching guidelines:
Use a white board on which four lines have been drawn. Use the cards from the appendix for word-building.

Teach word-building:
Select a word from the list below. Use only the letters needed to build that word and jumble them up. Ask the pupil to build that word by listening to the sounds in the words and segmenting all the sounds in the words, one at a time. The pupil then brings down each card once he/she has segmented the sound in the word. Ask the pupil to read the word he/she has built. Ask the pupil to write the word under the lines, saying the sounds as he/she writes each sound.

Word list for word-building, reading and spelling:
lost, held, silk, melt, bump, nest, hand, bend, lift, rant, desk, wilt, ramp, west, sent, loft, honk, help, milk, damp, junk, rift, bond, tank, pond, wind, vest, yelp, zest, kept, tilt, cost, dust, lamp

Book 1: Reading and spelling cvcc words

lost	✓	___ ___ ___ ___	
held		___ ___ ___ ___	
damp		___ ___ ___ ___	
milk		___ ___ ___ ___	
junk		___ ___ ___ ___	
hand		___ ___ ___ ___	
went		___ ___ ___ ___	
tilt		___ ___ ___ ___	
cost		___ ___ ___ ___	

Teaching aims: Reading and spelling cvcc words.

Teaching guidelines: Trim off this text box and fold the sheet along the dotted line. Ask the pupil to read the words on the left and tick the words she/he has read correctly. Ask the pupil to turn over the sheet. Dictate the words one at a time, encouraging the pupil to spell the words by segmenting and sounding out the sounds as she/he writes them. The pupil can then open the sheet and tick the words she/he has spelled correctly.

Words for dictation: lost held damp milk junk hand went tilt cost

pens
nips
pins

bunk
bank
sunk

vets
vats
vest

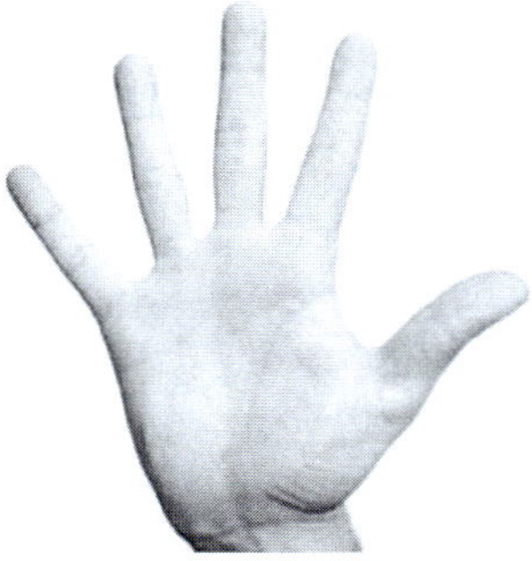

hand
bond
band

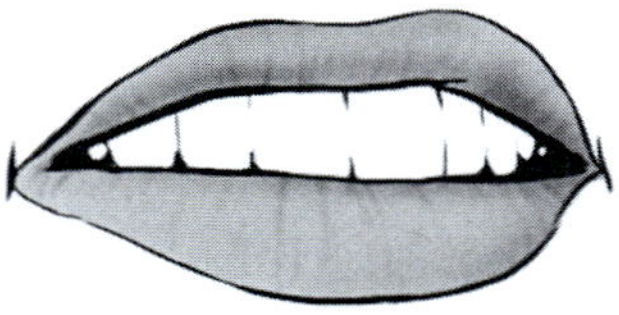

slip
lisp
lips

nods
pond
pops

Teaching aim: Reading accuracy

Teaching guidelines: Ask the pupil to read the words in each box and circle the word that matches the picture.

Book 1: Medial vowels (cvcc): Is it a real word?

a	e	i	o	u
d a m p ✔	d e m p ✘	d i m p ✘	d o m p ✘	d u m p ✔
l _ n d	l _ n d	l _ n d	l _ n d	l _ n d

a	e	i	o	u
h _ l p	h _ l p	h _ l p	h _ l p	h _ l p
t _ n t	t _ n t	t _ n t	t _ n t	t _ n t

a	e	i	o	u
g _ f t	g _ f t	g _ f t	g _ f t	g _ f t
f _ l m	f _ l m	f _ l m	f _ l m	f _ l m

Teaching aim: Reading accuracy

Teaching guidelines: Cut this sheet into three horizontal strips. Ask the pupil to insert the vowel sound into the space in each word and blend the sounds to read the word. Put a tick next to a real word and a cross next to a nonsense word.

Book 1: Reading practice cvcc words

band	disk	rest
wind	belt	gulp
camp	hulk	lift
rust	nest	pond
help	kept	kilt
mend	tank	sank
vest	wept	cvcc words (Alba Book 1)

Teaching aim: Reading practice

Teaching guidelines: Photocopy this page onto card and cut into reading cards

Book 1: Reading and spelling
Two-syllable words (cvcc level)

coll/ect	✓	_ _ _ _/_ _ _	
ant/hill		_ _ _/_ _ _ _	
desk/top		_ _ _ _/_ _ _	
pen/dant		_ _ _/_ _ _ _	
con/text		_ _ _/_ _ _ _	
con/vict		_ _ _/_ _ _ _	
ex/ist		_ _/_ _ _	
in/vent		_ _/_ _ _ _	
help/less		_ _ _ _/_ _ _ _	

Teaching aims: Reading and spelling words with vcc and cvcc syllables.

Teaching guidelines: Fold this sheet along the dotted line. Ask the pupil to read the words on the left and tick the words she/he has read correctly. Ask the pupil to turn over the sheet and dictate the words to the pupil. Ask the pupil to spell the words by segmenting and sounding out the sounds as she/he writes them on the lines. Ask the pupil to open the sheet and tick the words she/he has spelled correctly.

Book 1: Reading practice
Two-syllable words (cvcc level)

consent	windmill	exact
insult	subject	dentist
desktop	batsman	sandpit
dustbin	collect	handbag
absent	arrest	suspect
adopt	forest	invent
contact	adult	Two-syllable words cvcc level (Alba Book 1)

Teaching aim: Reading practice

Teaching guidelines: Photocopy this page onto card and cut into reading cards

Book 1: 4-in-a-row game (cvcc)

mend	lift	pump	hand	hunt
gulp	lost	dent	bond	band
wind	rent	dust	land	rest
sank	soft	gift	wept	vest
silk	sand	tank	font	rust
best	sink	nest	loft	kept
belt	mint	musk	honk	bank

A game for two players: Play with two sets of coloured counters. Players take turns to read a word and put a counter on it. The winner is the first to get four of his or her counters in a row in any direction. The winner places a counter on an apple symbol. The game is played four times until all the apple symbols are covered.

Book 1: Stepping stones reading game (cvcc) words

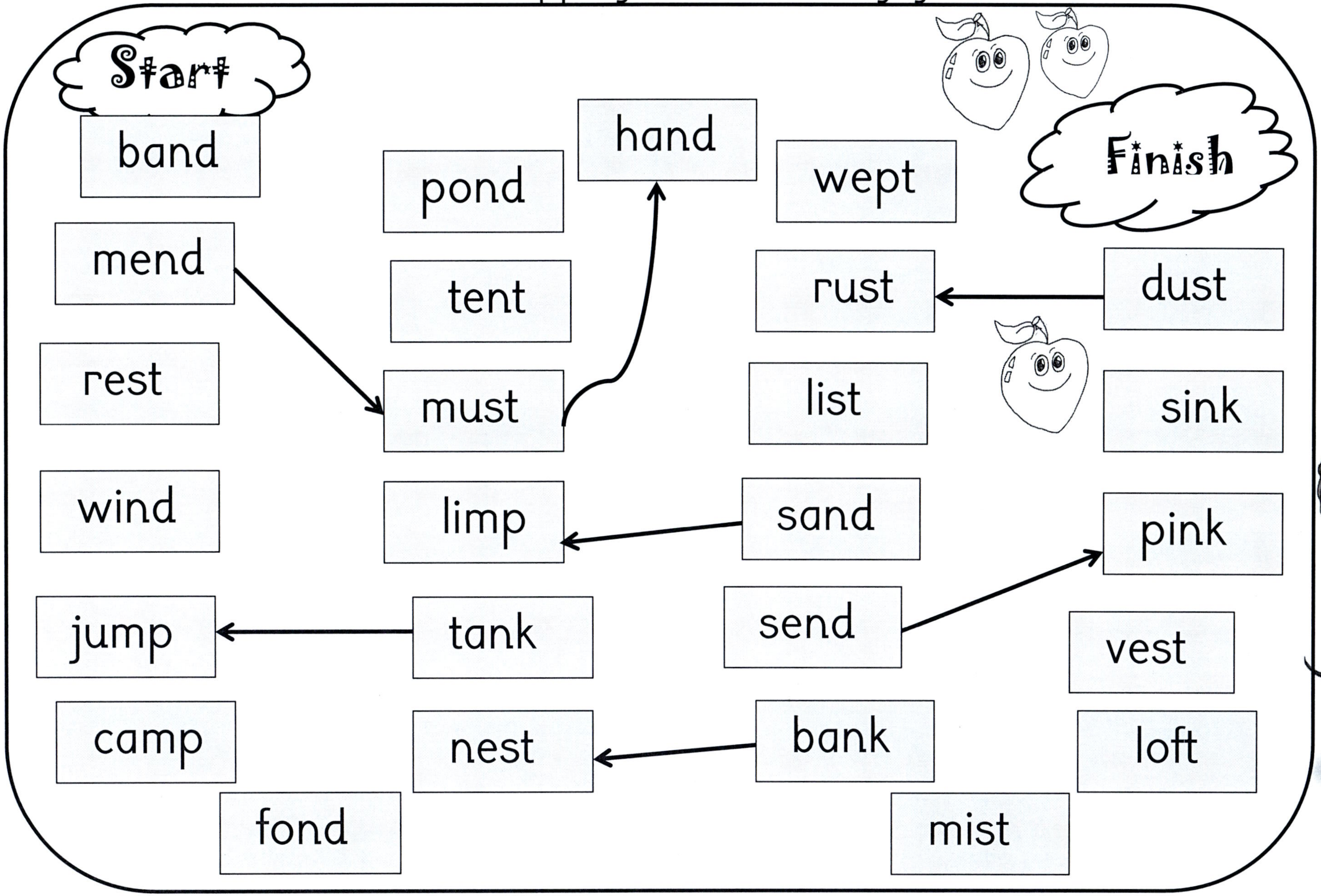

A game for 1–4 players: Play with counters and dice.
Players should read aloud the words that they land on at the end of each turn and follow the direction arrows if they land on them.

Book 1: Questions for discussion

Chapter 1

1. Is Alba at the lab when the story starts? (page 1)
2. What has happened to the apple trees? (page 2)
3. Why does Max, at the lab, want to steal the last apple pip? (page 3)

Chapter 2

1. What does Alba do when she sees the man at the flat? (page 5)
2. Why can't the man catch her? (page 7)

Chapter 3

1. Where does Alba find to hide? (page 8)
2. What does she do with the last apple pip? (page 9)

Chapter 4

1. Who comes to the hut? (page 10)
2. What happens to Alba? (page 10)
3. Does Max get the last apple pip? (page 11)

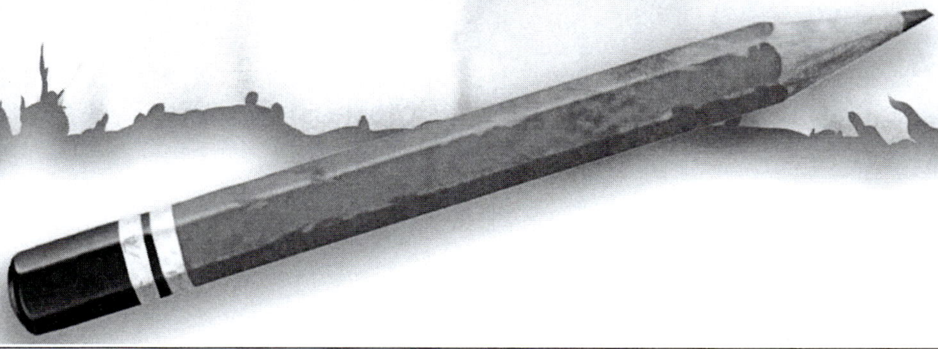

Teaching aims: Speaking and listening skills, comprehension and vocabulary

Teaching guidelines: These questions can be discussed after reading the text

Book 1: True or false?

	yes	no
Alba is at the lab with her dad.		
A bad man plans to sell the last pip.		
Alba grabs the pip and runs from the flat.		
Alba gets on a bus.		
Alba runs into a hut.		
Alba's dog, Ben, is in the hut.		
Alba is as big as a tin can.		
Max gets the last pip.		

Teaching aim: Comprehension

Teaching guidelines: Ask the pupil to read the sentences and tick the boxes according to whether they are true or false.

Book 1: Picture the scene

Alba is as big as the cup.

She is next to the cup.

The cup has a sun on it.

Next to the cup is a big cobweb.

Teaching aims: Following instructions, comprehension and vocabulary

Teaching guidelines: Encourage the pupil to read the text carefully and draw the details of the picture as described in the text.

Book 1: Alba's diary

I am as big as a tin can! I have a pip in the bag.

It is the last pip. I must rest until Dad sends help.

I ___ ___ ___ ___ ___ ___ ___

___ ___ a ___ ___ ___ ___ ___ ___!

I have a ___ ___ ___ ___ ___

the ___ ___ ___. ___ ___ is the

___ ___ ___ ___ ___ ___ ___.

I ___ ___ ___ ___ ___ ___ ___ ___

___ ___ ___ ___ ___ ___ ___ ___

sends ___ ___ ___ ___.

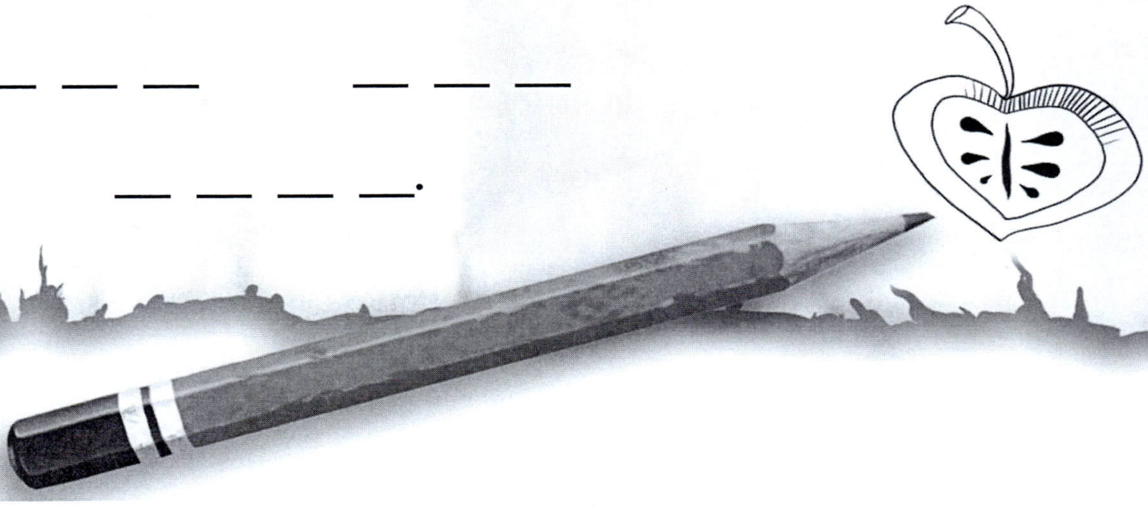

Teaching aims: Reading and spelling activity
Teaching guidelines: Encourage the pupil to copy the text at the top and insert it into the cloze exercise below it. Pupils should write a sound on each line e.g: h e l p. This activity can also be used for dictation.

Book 1: New words

New words in Book 1

sips – drinks a little at a time
a limp – an uneven walk caused by a weak or injured leg
tugs – pulls hard at something
jabs – pokes hard

REMINDER – A sentence **begins** with a capital letter and **ends** with a full stop.

Alba tugs at the rug	a cup of milk.

Alba sips	and cannot run.

The man at the lab plans	the red pen at Alba.

The man has a limp	so it is on top of the bag.

The man jabs	to sell the last pip.

Teaching aims: This activity includes new vocabulary introduced in Book 1. It encourages the pupil to think about the meaning of the new words and to use them to construct a complete sentence.
Teaching guidelines: Cut the sentences into strips and cut along the centre line. Ask the pupil to match the two parts of the sentence so that they make sense. The pupil may need a reminder of what the words mean.

Book 1: Postcard home

Dear Mum,

First

Then

In the end

Love from Alba xxx

Teaching aims: Comprehension and free writing

Teaching guidelines: Encourage the pupil to write about what happened in Book 1. The sentence starters provide useful cues for breaking the story into sections. Useful words are provided at the bottom of the page. The teacher can decide whether or not to offer these.

Useful words: Max run bag pip grab man hut tin can

Book 1: Punctuation

Capital letters and full stops

REMINDER – A sentence **begins** with a capital letter and **ends** with a full stop.

the last pip is in a box at the flat dad is at the lab a bad man has a plan to get the pip

the man has a fat red pen the pen hits alba in the ribs

alba is as big as a tin can she runs and sits next to the rug the pip is in the rug alba must rest next to the pip

Did you spot?

9 missing full stops

10 missing capital letters

Book 2: The Plan

Phonic focus: ccvc **Spellings:** ccvc words

Contents

Book 2: Word-building ccvc words

c	r	a	b
c	*r*	*a*	*b*

Teaching aims:

- Segment and blend ccvc (consonant/consonant/vowel/consonant) words with the sounds of the alphabet and double consonants.

Teaching guidelines:
Use a white board on which four lines have been drawn. Use the cards from the introductory levels.

Teach word-building:
Select a word from the list below. Use only the letters needed to build that word and jumble them up. Ask the pupil to build that word by listening to the sounds in the words and segmenting all the sounds in the words, one at a time. The pupil then brings down each card once he/she has segmented the sound in the word. Ask the pupil to read the word he/she has built. Ask the pupil to write the word under the lines, saying the sounds as he/she writes each sound.

Word list for word-building, reading and spelling:
Crab, slip, stop, grub, sled, plum, snap, step, from, blip, drip, drag, stun, pram, gran, drug, slap, blob, flan, snip, bled, fret, slam, blot, drop, tram, slot, plot, trot, brag, clan, glen, flip

stem	✓	___ ___ ___ ___	
drip		___ ___ ___ ___	
step		___ ___ ___ ___	
plot		___ ___ ___ ___	
glug		___ ___ ___ ___	
bran		___ ___ ___ ___	
crab		___ ___ ___ ___	
trim		___ ___ ___ ___	
slop		___ ___ ___ ___	

Teaching aims: Reading and spelling ccvc words.

Teaching guidelines: Trim off this text box and fold the sheet along the dotted line. Ask the pupil to read the words on the left and tick the words she/he has read correctly. Ask the pupil to turn over the sheet. Dictate the words one at a time, encouraging the pupil to spell the words by segmenting and sounding out the sounds as she/he writes them. The pupil can then open the sheet and tick the words she/he has spelled correctly.

Words for dictation: stem drip step plot glug bran crab trim slop

Book 2: Reading accuracy ccvc words

flag

flog

flab

crib

crab

crop

from

flog

frog

sold

sled

slot

lump

pulp

plum

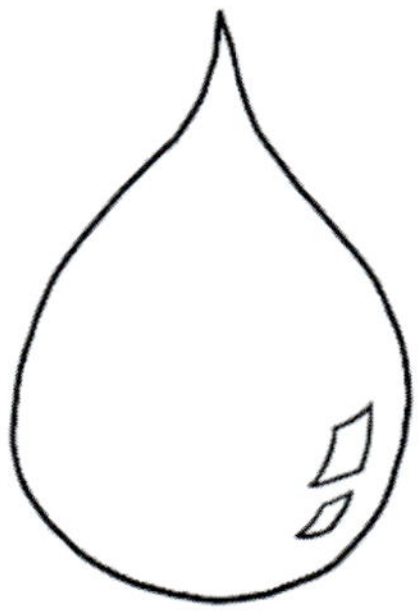

drag

drop

drug

Teaching aim: Reading accuracy

Teaching guidelines: Ask the pupil to read the words in each box and circle the word that matches the picture.

Book 2: Medial vowels (ccvc): Is it a real word?

a	e	i	o	u
g l a d ✓	g l e d ✗	g l i d ✗	g l o d ✗	g l u d ✗
s p _ n	s p _ n	s p _ n	s p _ n	s p _ n

a	e	i	o	u
p r _ m	p r _ m	p r _ m	p r _ m	p r _ m
g r _ n	g r _ n	g r _ n	g r _ n	g r _ n

a	e	i	o	u
f l _ p	f l _ p	f l _ p	f l _ p	f l _ p
s t _ p	s t _ p	s t _ p	s t _ p	s t _ p

Teaching aim: Reading accuracy

Teaching guidelines: Cut this sheet into three horizontal strips. Ask the pupil to insert the vowel sound into the space in each word and blend the sounds to read the word. Put a tick next to a real word and a cross next to a nonsense word.

Book 2: Reading practice ccvc words

brag	club	dress
flat	grim	plot
scan	slog	trek
snag	twig	flex
crop	sled	smog
scum	glen	skip
sniff	spell	ccvc words (Alba Book 2)

Teaching aim: Reading practice

Teaching guidelines: Photocopy this page onto card and cut into reading cards.

Book 2: Reading and spelling
Two-syllable words (ccvc level)

frog/man	✓	___ ___ ___ ___/___ ___ ___	
com/plex		___ ___ ___/___ ___ ___ ___	
cred/it		___ ___ ___ ___/___ ___	
frag/ment		___ ___ ___ ___/___ ___ ___ ___	
drop/lets		___ ___ ___ ___/___ ___ ___ ___	
un/dress		___ ___/___ ___ ___ ___	
trip/let		___ ___ ___ ___/___ ___ ___	
stun/gun		___ ___ ___ ___/___ ___ ___	
in/step		___ ___/___ ___ ___ ___	

Teaching aims: Reading and spelling words with ccvc syllables.

Teaching guidelines: Fold this sheet along the dotted line. Ask the pupil to read the words on the left and tick the words she/he has read correctly. Ask the pupil to turn over the sheet and dictate the words to the pupil. Ask the pupil to spell the words by segmenting and sounding out the sounds as she/he writes them on the lines. Ask the pupil to open the sheet and tick the words she/he has spelled correctly.

Book 2: Reading practice
Two-syllable words (ccvc level)

trumpet	fabric	dandruff
nonstop	picnic	across
undress	frogman	drastic
profit	crumpet	credit
express	complex	project
driven	fragment	plastic
snippet	frantic	Two-syllable words ccvc level (Alba Book 2)

Teaching aim: Reading practice

Teaching guidelines: Photocopy this page onto card and cut into reading cards

Book 2: 4–in–a–row game (ccvc)

club	stop	slam	twig	brag
gran	drum	clap	blot	swam
prod	grin	from	crab	flag
grab	plum	spell	smug	cress
dwell	frill	glad	pram	skip
slug	spot	trip	slim	snug
dress	skid	drag	stag	step

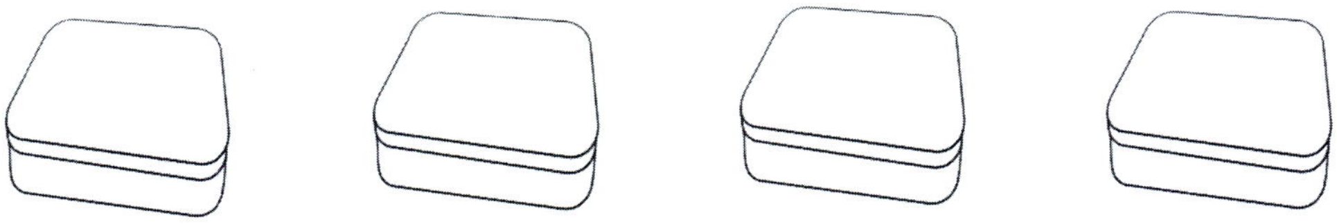

A game for two players: Play with two sets of coloured counters. Players take turns to read a word and put a counter on it. The winner is the first to get four of his or her counters in a row in any direction. The winner places a counter on a box symbol. The game is played four times until all the box symbols are covered.

Book 2: Stepping stones reading game (ccvc) words

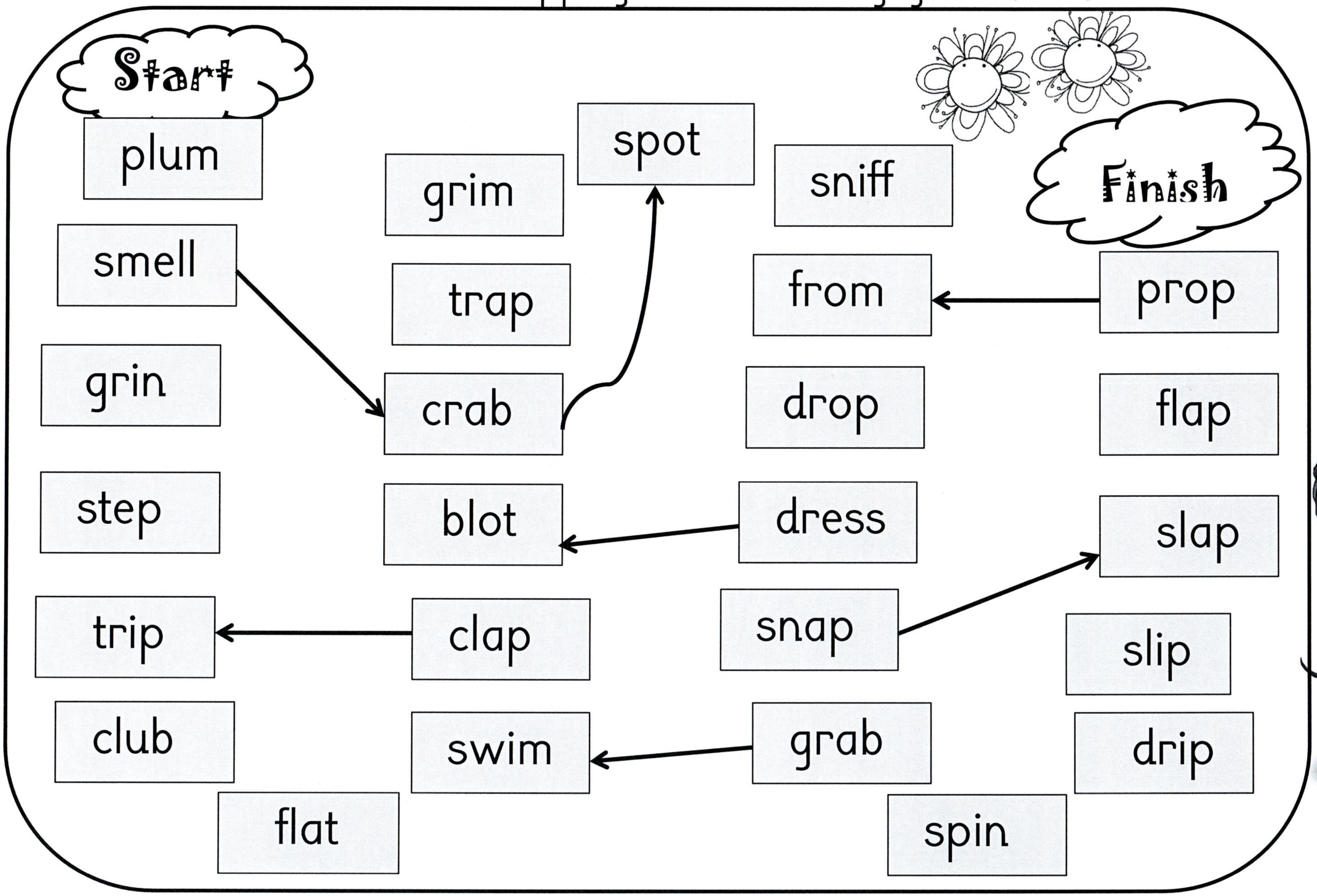

A game for 1–4 players: Play with counters and dice.
Players should read aloud the words that they land on at the end of each turn and follow the direction arrows if they land on them.

Book 2: Questions for discussion

Chapter 1

1. Why does Alba want to get into her bag? (page 2)
2. How does she feel about being 10cm tall? (page 3)

Chapter 2

1. What is Alba's plan? (page 4)
2. Why can't she get the box to Dad? (page 5)

Chapter 3

1. Why does Alba make a bag? (page 7)

Chapter 4

1. Why does Alba want to get the map from her bag? (page 9)
2. What route does Alba plan with the map? (page 11)
3. Why does Alba hold on tightly to the bag with the pip in while she goes to sleep? (page 12)

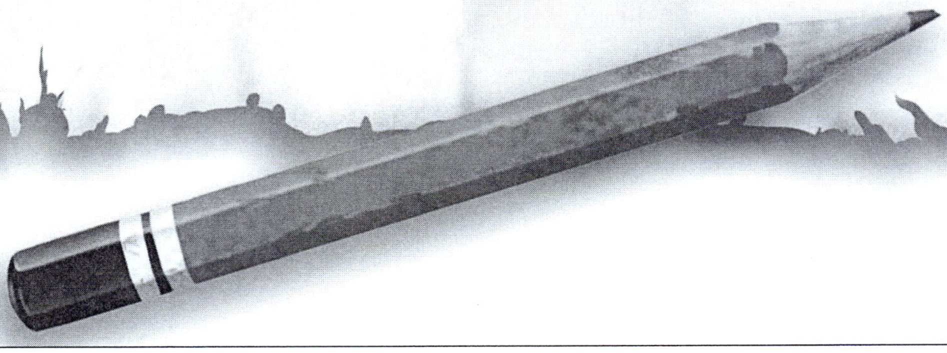

Teaching aims: Speaking and listening skills, comprehension and vocabulary.

Teaching guidelines: These questions can be discussed after reading the text.

Book 2: True or false?

	yes	no
Alba has a rest in a tin can.		
Alba has a bun in her bag.		
Alba has milk in her bag.		
The last pip is lost in the dust.		
The box with the pip in is as big as a bed.		
Dad sends help.		
The map helps Alba.		
In the end, Alba has still not got a plan.		

Teaching aim: Comprehension
Teaching guidelines: Ask the pupil to read the sentences and tick the boxes according to whether they are true or false.

Book 2: Picture the scene

Alba has the map as a tent.

The box is next to her.

The pip is in the box.

Alba has a scrap of soft rug to rest on.

Teaching aims: Following instructions, comprehension and vocabulary

Teaching guidelines: Encourage the pupil to read the text carefully and draw the details of the picture as described in the text.

Book 2: Alba's diary

I can get the pip to Dad. I have the pip in a bag and a map. I will rest until I am fit and can run.

I ___ ___ ___ ___ ___ ___ the

___ ___ ___ to ___ ___ ___. I have

the ___ ___ ___ ___ ___ a ___ ___ ___

___ ___ ___ a ___ ___ ___.

I ___ ___ ____ ___ ___ ___ ___ until

I ___ ___ ___ ___ ___ ___ ___ ___

___ ___ ___ ___ ___ ___.

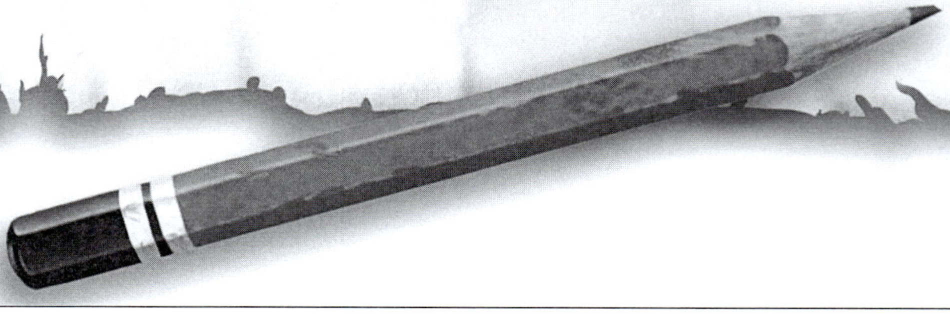

Teaching aims: Reading and spelling activity
Teaching guidelines: Encourage the pupil to copy the text at the top and insert it into the cloze exercise below it. Pupils should write a sound on each line e.g: w i ll. Remind the pupil that some sounds are spelled with more than one letter and that these sounds will have longer lines. This activity can also be used for dictation.

Book 2: New words

New words in Book 2

strap – a strip of material used as a handle
limp – tired and lacking energy
gulps – swallows
skids – slides along
prop – something to lean against that gives support

REMINDER – A sentence **begins** with a capital letter and **ends** with a full stop.

Alba is hot	a box of milk.

Alba skids	and limp.

Alba gulps at	across the map.

The lid of the box	the strap of the bag.

Alba holds	is a prop.

Teaching aims: This activity includes new vocabulary introduced in Book 2. It encourages the pupil to think about the meaning of the new words and to use them to construct a complete sentence.
Teaching guidelines: Cut the sentences into strips and cut along the centre line. Ask the pupil to match the two parts of the sentence so that they make sense. The pupil may need a reminder of what the words mean.

Book 2: Postcard home

Dear Mum,

First

Then

In the end

Love from Alba xxx

Teaching aims: Comprehension and free writing

Teaching guidelines: Encourage the pupil to write about what happened in Book 2. The sentence starters provide useful cues for breaking the story into sections. Useful words are provided at the bottom of the page. The teacher can decide whether or not to offer these.

Useful words: box rest milk bed map plan across

Book 2: Punctuation

Capital letters and full stops

REMINDER – A sentence **begins** with a capital letter and **ends** with a full stop.

alba is hot and sad she gets milk from her bag she is sad she is as big as a tin can

alba gets the pip from the bag the box is as big as a bed she has to get the pip to her dad

alba drags the lid off the box and gets the pip she gets a scrap of cloth the pip is snug in a bag and alba can rest

Did you spot?

10 *missing full stops*

11 *missing capital letters*

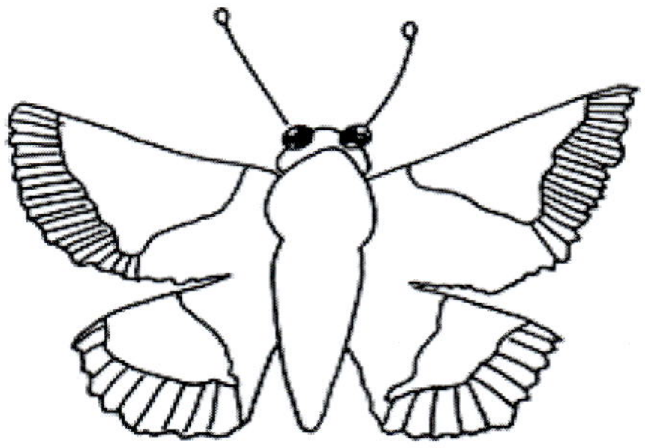

Book 3: Alba Slips Up

Phonic focus: ccvcc **Spellings:** ccvcc words

Contents

Book 3: Word–building ccvcc words

f	l	a	g	s
f	*l*	*a*	*g*	*s*

Teaching aims:

- Segment and blend ccvcc (consonant/consonant/vowel/consonant/consonant) words with the sounds of the alphabet.

Teaching guidelines:
Use a white board on which four lines have been drawn. Use the cards from the appendix for word–building.

Teach word–building:
Select a word from the list below. Use only the letters needed to build that word and jumble them up. Ask the pupil to build that word by listening to the sounds in the words and segmenting all the sounds in the words, one at a time. The pupil then brings down each card once he/she has segmented the sound in the word. Ask the pupil to read the word he/she has built. Ask the pupil to write the word under the lines, saying the sounds as he/she writes each sound.

Word list for word–building, reading and spelling:
flags, drank, swift, smelt, blond, tramp, plank, slump, slots, drips, stand, skunk, plump, grand, trump, crisp, trend, frost, grunt, twins, trust, bland, brand, clamp, print, prank, steps, stump

Book 3: Reading and spelling ccvcc words

flags	✓	_ _ _ _ _	
drink		_ _ _ _ _	
slump		_ _ _ _ _	
spots		_ _ _ _ _	
print		_ _ _ _ _	
frost		_ _ _ _ _	
trend		_ _ _ _ _	
crisp		_ _ _ _ _	
clamp		_ _ _ _ _	

Teaching aims: Reading and spelling ccvcc words.

Teaching guidelines: Fold this sheet along the dotted line. Ask the pupil to read the words on the left and tick the words she/he has read correctly. Ask the pupil to turn over the sheet and dictate the words to the pupil. Ask the pupil to spell the words by segmenting and sounding out the sounds as she/he writes them on the lines. Ask the pupil to open the sheet and tick the words she/he has spelled correctly.

Words for dictation: flags drink slump spots print frost trend crisp clamp

Book 3: Reading accuracy ccvcc words

pets
spells
steps

pomp
stamp
stomp

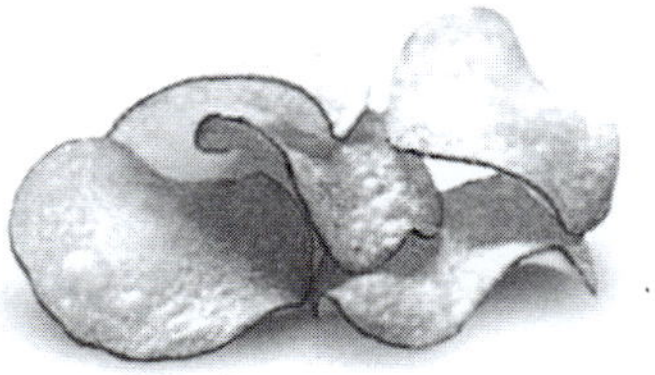

crisps
cribs
brick

flags
glass
lags

stops
spits
spots

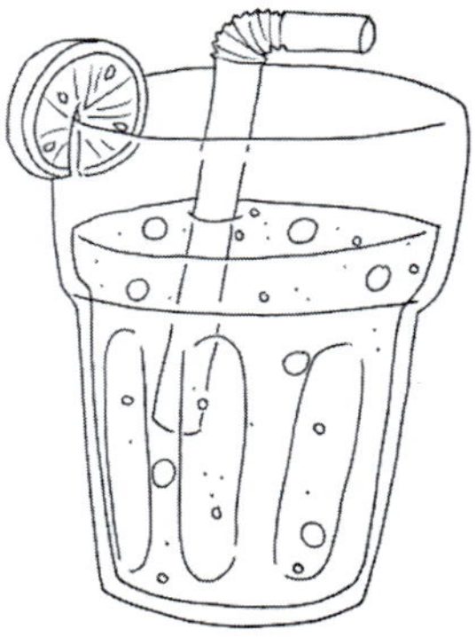

brink
drink
blank

Teaching aim: Reading accuracy

Teaching guidelines: Ask the pupil to read the words in each box and circle the word that matches the picture.

Book 3: Reading practice ccvcc words

grand	spots	stamp
blend	crept	trust
blank	steps	twist
croft	brisk	snaps
clump	drink	frost
spent	spins	stand
spelt	croft	ccvcc words (Alba Book 3)

Teaching aim: Reading practice

Teaching guidelines: Photocopy this page onto card and cut into reading cards.

Book 3: Reading practice

Two-syllable words with ccvcc in one of the syllables

con tract	blank et	ex tinct
splend id	trans fix	stunt man
frost ed	un clamp	con tests
Two-syllable words with ccvcc spellings (Alba Book 3)		Two-syllable words with ccvcc spellings (Syllables split) (Alba Book 3)
contract	blanket	extinct
splendid	transfix	stuntman
frosted	unclamp	contests

Teaching aim: Reading practice

Teaching guidelines: Photocopy this page onto card and cut into reading cards. The teacher can decide whether to offer these words with the syllable split identified.

Book 3: 4–in–a–row game (ccvcc)

crept	blond	trust	stamp	flint
blank	steps	twist	croft	brisk
snaps	clump	drink	frost	spent
spins	stand	spelt	grand	spots
blink	trips	stink	slump	skips
trunk	clips	spend	spilt	traps
scalp	skunk	print	plank	crust

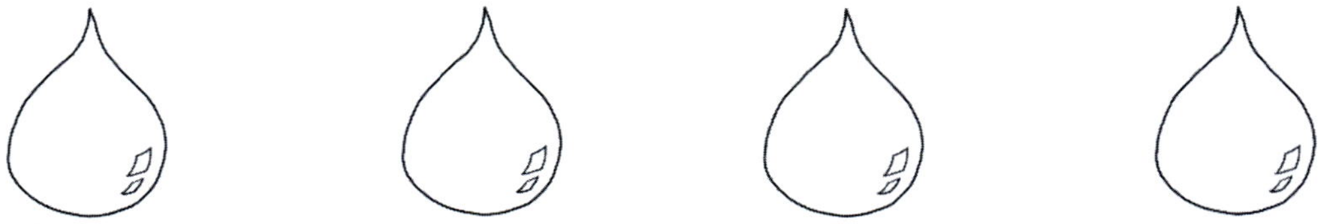

A game for two players: Play with two sets of coloured counters. Players take turns to read a word and put a counter on it. The winner is the first to get four of his or her counters in a row in any direction. The winner places a counter on a water symbol. The game is played four times until all the water symbols are covered.

Book 3: Stepping stones reading game (ccvcc) words

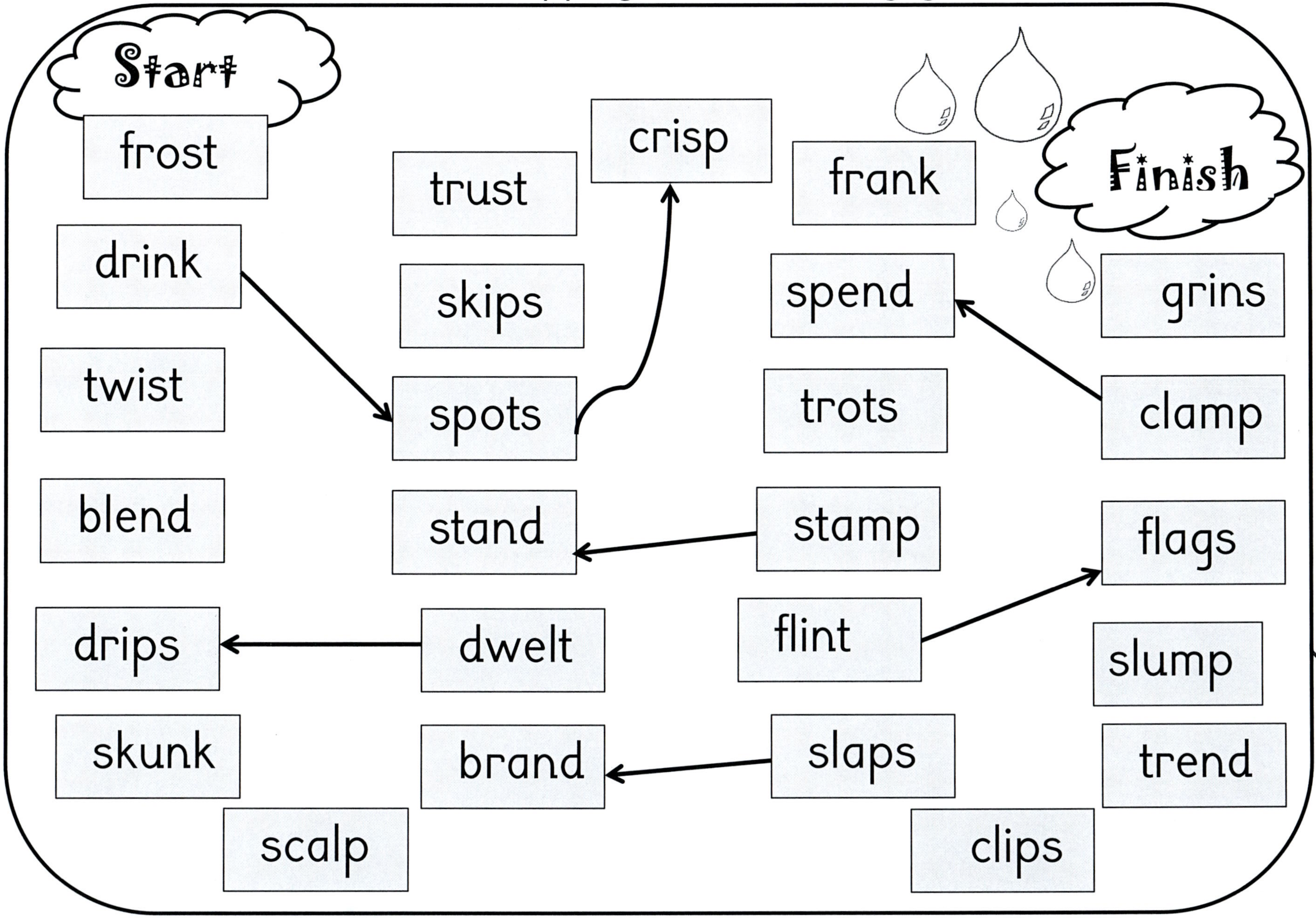

A game for 1–4 players: Play with counters and dice.
Players should read aloud the words that they land on at the end of each turn and follow the direction arrows if they land on them.

Book 3: Questions for discussion

Chapter 1

1. Why does Alba want to leave the hut? (page 1)
2. What is waiting outside the hut? (page 3)

Chapter 2

1. What happens when the dog chases Alba? (page 5)
2. Why does the dog leave? (page 7)
3. How does Alba get across the pit of mud? (page 7)

Chapter 3

1. Alba hopes the water from the tap will help her solve two problems. What are those problems? (page 10)
2. How does Alba get a drink from the tap? (page 10)

Chapter 4

3. Does Alba lose the last apple pip in the pit of mud? (page 12)

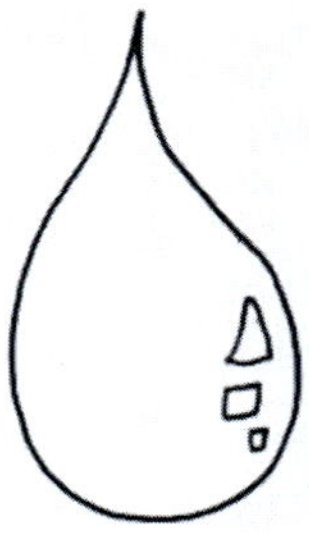

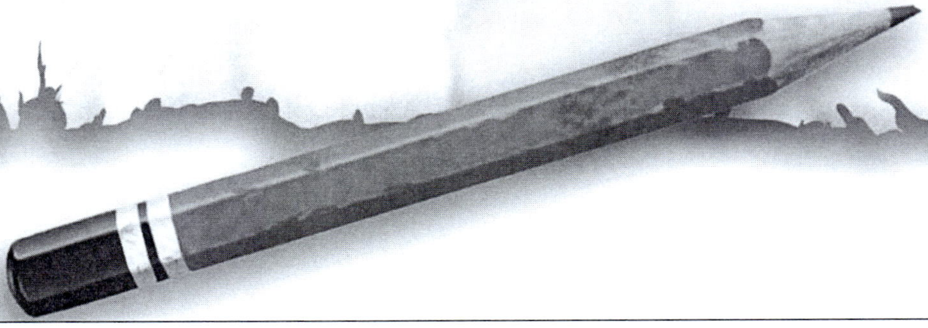

Teaching aims: Speaking and listening skills, comprehension and vocabulary.

Teaching guidelines: These questions can be discussed after reading the text.

Book 3: True or false?

	yes	no
Alba has to get back to the flat.		
A big, plump pig is next to the hut.		
Alba slips in a pit of wet mud.		
Alba grabs hold of a twig.		
The twig slips from her grip.		
Alba can jump from twig to twig.		
The tap is stiff with rust.		
Alba sips milk in the hot sun.		

Teaching aim: Comprehension
Teaching guidelines: Ask the pupil to read the sentences and tick the boxes according to whether they are true or false.

Book 3: Picture the scene

Alba is on top of a twig.

The twig is in a pit of mud.

The mud has six twigs on top.

Alba has the bag with the pip in her hand.

Alba has a lot of mud on her leg.

Teaching aims: Following instructions, comprehension and vocabulary

Teaching guidelines: Encourage the pupil to read the text carefully and draw the details of the picture as described in the text.

Book 3: Alba's diary

A big, plump dog ran at me. I fell in the mud and it stank! I got on top of a twig and got to the end of the mud. The pip is wet but not lost. It is still snug in the bag.

A _ _ _, _ _ _ _ _ _ _ _

_ _ _ _ _ me. I _ _ _

_ _ the _ _ _ _ _ _ _ _

_ _ _ _ _! I _ _ _ _ _

_ _ _ of a _ _ _ _ _ _ _

_ _ _ to the _ _ _ of the

_ _ _. The _ _ _ _ _

_ _ _ _ _ _ _ _ _ _ _ _ _.

_ _ is _ _ _ _

_ _ _ _ _ _ the _ _ _.

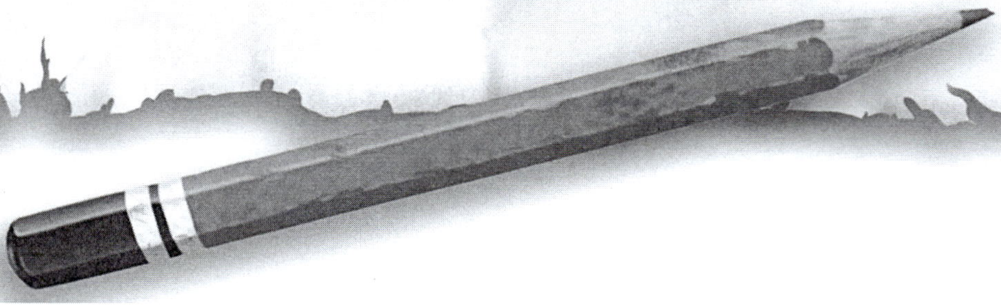

Teaching aims: Reading and spelling activity
Teaching guidelines: Encourage the pupil to copy the text at the top and insert it into the cloze exercise below it. Pupils should write a sound on each line e.g: h e l p. This activity can also be used for dictation.

Book 3: New words

New words in Book 3

swift – able to move quickly
prods – pokes or jabs
snug – warm and cosy
grunts – makes a deep guttural sound in the throat
plump – chubby or fleshy

REMINDER – A sentence **begins** with a capital letter and **ends** with a full stop.

A big, plump dog	and swift.

Alba prods	is still snug in the bag.

Alba is fit	the damp bag.

The big dog stands up	rests next to the hut.

The pip	with a grunt.

Teaching aims: This activity includes new vocabulary introduced in Book 3. It encourages the pupil to think about the meaning of the new words and to use them to construct a complete sentence.
Teaching guidelines: Cut the sentences into strips and cut along the centre line. Ask the pupil to match the two parts of the sentence so that they make sense. The pupil may need a reminder of what the words mean.

Book 3: Postcard home

Dear Mum,

First

Then

In the end

Love from Alba xxx

Teaching aims: Comprehension and free writing

Teaching guidelines: Encourage the pupil to write about what happened in Book 3. The sentence starters provide useful cues for breaking the story into sections. Useful words are provided at the bottom of the page. The teacher can decide whether or not to offer these.

Useful words: plump rests slips grabs twig rust twists

Book 3: Punctuation

Capital letters and full stops

REMINDER – A sentence **begins** with a capital letter and **ends** with a full stop.

alba must get the pip to the lab she has no milk left to drink

a big plump dog is next to the hut he can smell alba he drops spit from his wet lips as he sniffs

alba slips in the wet mud the mud is cold and it stinks she grabs a twig and jumps from twig to twig the pip gets wet but it is still snug in the bag

Did you spot?

9 missing full stops

10 missing capital

Book 4: Hot Chips for Lunch

Phonic focus: 'sh' 'ch' 'th' **Spellings:** sh ch tch th

Contents

Book 4: Word-building with ‘ch’

ch	i	p
ch	i	p

Teaching aims:

- Learn the sound ‘ch’ and the corresponding spellings: <ch> and <tch>
- Segment and blend words with the sound ‘ch’

Teaching guidelines:

Use a white board on which three lines have been drawn. Print cards from the appendix for the spellings <ch> and <tch>. Add them to the cards with the letters of the alphabet from previous levels.

1. Teach word-building with the spelling <ch>:

First teach the spelling <ch>. Select a word from the list below. Use only the letters needed to build that word and jumble them up. Ask the pupil to build that word by listening to the sounds in the words and segmenting all the sounds in the words, one at a time. The pupil then brings down each card once he/she has segmented the sound in the word. Ask the pupil to read the word he/she has built. Ask the pupil to write the word under the lines, saying the sounds as he/she writes each sound. Draw more lines for longer words.

2. Teach word-building with the spelling <tch>:

Follow the steps above with the spelling <tch>.

Word list for word-building, reading and spelling:

<ch>: chat, chess, chill, chin, chop, chum, chunk, chimp, much, such, inch, rich, bench, lunch
<tch>: fetch, patch, titch, hutch, catch, glitch, stitch, hatch, snitch, pitch, ditch, clutch, Dutch

f	e	tch
f	e	tch

chip	✓	___ ___ ___	
chess		___ ___ ___	
chin		___ ___ ___	
much		___ ___ ___	
bench		___ ___ ___ ___	
lunch		___ ___ ___ ___	
catch		___ ___ ___	
ditch		___ ___ ___	
hutch		___ ___ ___	

Teaching aims: Reading and spelling words with the spellings <ch> and <tch> for the sound 'ch'.

Teaching guidelines: Fold this sheet along the dotted line. Ask the pupil to read the words on the left and tick the words she/he has read correctly. Ask the pupil to turn over the sheet and dictate the words to the pupil. Ask the pupil to spell the words by segmenting and sounding out the sounds as she/he writes them on the lines. Ask the pupil to open the sheet and tick the words she/he has spelled correctly.

Book 4: Reading accuracy 'ch' words

chimp
chomp
champ

pitch
Dutch
hutch

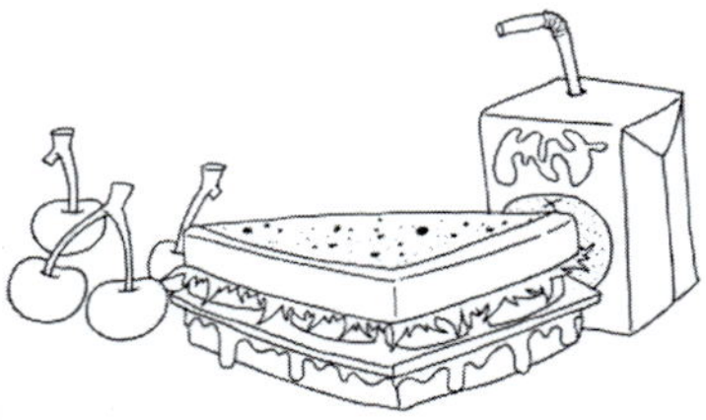

hunch
lunch
chunk

stitch
titch
ditch

chops
chums
chips

bunch
bench
pinch

Teaching aim: Reading accuracy

Teaching guidelines: Ask the pupil to read the words in each box and circle the word that matches the picture.

Book 4: Reading practice

<ch> and <tch> words

chat	much	catch
inch	pitch	chips
fetch	bench	chess
rich	lunch	ditch
latch	finch	chunk
chill	chimp	chap
chest	hutch	Words with <ch> and <tch> (Alba Book 4)

Teaching aim: Reading practice

Teaching guidelines: Photocopy this page onto card and cut into reading cards.

Book 4: Reading and spelling

Two-syllable words with <ch> and <tch> spellings

chip/munk	✓	___ ___ ___/___ ___ ___ ___	
lunch/box		___ ___ ___ ___/___ ___ ___	
chaff/inch		___ ___ ___/___ ___ ___	
chin/strap		___ ___ ___/___ ___ ___ ___ ___	
rich/ness		___ ___ ___/___ ___ ___	
ost/rich		___ ___ ___/___ ___ ___	
chest/nut		___ ___ ___ ___/___ ___ ___	
match/box		___ ___ ___/___ ___ ___	
hatch/et		___ ___ ___ /___ ___	

Teaching aims: Reading and spelling words with <ch and tch> spellings.

Teaching guidelines: Fold this sheet along the dotted line. Ask the pupil to read the words on the left and tick the words she/he has read correctly. Ask the pupil to turn over the sheet and dictate the words to the pupil. Ask the pupil to spell the words by segmenting and sounding out the sounds as she/he writes them on the lines. Ask the pupil to open the sheet and tick the words she/he has spelled correctly.

Book 4: Reading practice

Two-syllable words with <ch> and <tch>

chinstrap	chatting	chipmunk
matching	chestnut	lunchbox
richness	ostrich	matchbox
hatchet	chopping	children
dispatch	attach	hopscotch
mismatch	topstitch	clenching
fetching	ketchup	Two-syllable words with <ch> and <tch> (Alba Book 4)

Teaching aim: Reading practice

Teaching guidelines: Photocopy this page onto card and cut into reading cards

Book 4: 4-in-a-row game 'ch'

chat	much	chin	inch	chop
chips	chum	chess	ditch	lunch
such	finch	chunk	chill	chimp
hutch	latch	chest	bunch	rich
champ	batch	munch	hunch	bench
crunch	stitch	hatch	snitch	clutch
pinch	Dutch	patch	punch	chip

A game for two players: Play with two sets of coloured counters. Players take turns to read a word and put a counter on it. The winner is the first to get four of his or her counters in a row in any direction. The winner places a counter on a chips symbol. The game is played four times until all the chips symbols are covered.

Book 4: Stepping stones reading game 'ch' words

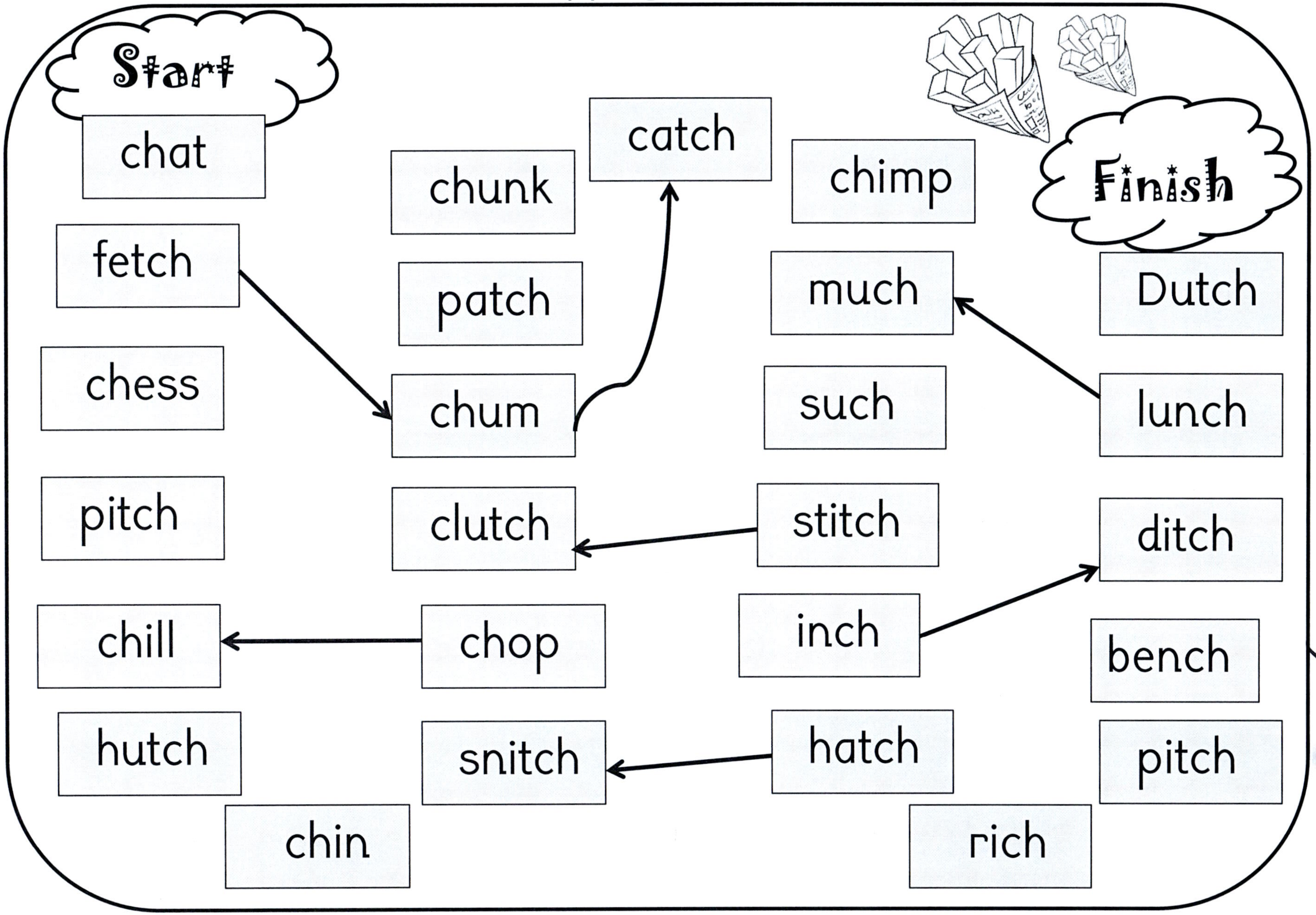

A game for 1–4 players: Play with counters and dice.
Players should read aloud the words that they land on at the end of each turn and follow the direction arrows if they land on them.

Book 4: Word-building with 'sh'

sh	o	p
sh	*o*	*p*

Teaching aims:

- learn the sound 'sh' and the corresponding spelling <sh>
- be able to segment and blend words with 'sh'

Teaching guidelines:
Use a white board on which three lines have been drawn. Print a card from the appendix for the spelling <sh>. Add it to the cards with the letters of the alphabet from previous levels.

Teach word-building with the spelling <sh>:
Select a word from the list below. Use only the letters needed to build that word and jumble them up. Ask the pupil to build that word by listening to the sounds in the words and segmenting all the sounds in the words, one at a time. The pupil then brings down each card once he/she has segmented the sound in the word. Ask the pupil to read the word he/she has built. Ask the pupil to write the word under the lines, saying the sounds as he/she writes each sound. Draw more lines for longer words.

Word list for word-building, reading and spelling:
Shop, shed, shin, shut, ship, shall, shell, shift, shred, shot, rush, gash, wish, dash, fish, dish, posh, hush, bash, crash, smash, splash, clash, brash, shrub, shrug, brush, shelf

shop	✓	___ ___ ___	
shell		___ ___ ___	
shut		___ ___ ___	
wish		___ ___ ___	
hush		___ ___ ___	
dash		___ ___ ___	
brush		___ ___ ___ ___	
smash		___ ___ ___ ___	
shrug		___ ___ ___ ___	

Teaching aims: Reading and spelling words with 'sh'.

Teaching guidelines: Fold this sheet along the dotted line. Ask the pupil to read the words on the left and tick the words she/he has read correctly. Ask the pupil to turn over the sheet and dictate the words to the pupil. Ask the pupil to spell the words by segmenting and sounding out the sounds as she/he writes them on the lines. Ask the pupil to open the sheet and tick the words she/he has spelled correctly.

Book 4: Reading accuracy 'sh' words

ship
shin
shun

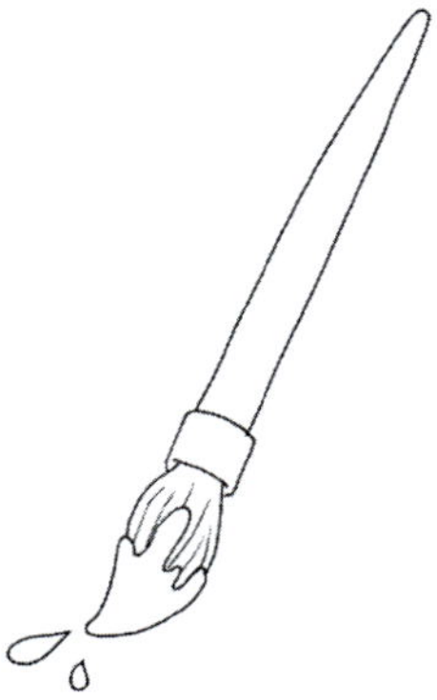

shrub
crush
brush

shop
shot
shut

shelf
shank
shrimp

fish
wish
slush

shrug
shed
shin

Teaching aim: Reading accuracy

Teaching guidelines: Ask the pupil to read the words in each box and circle the word that matches the picture.

rush	wish	splash
shed	shin	shell
shop	shut	shall
shelf	shrub	shift
cash	shunt	shrug
brush	fish	rash
shrimp	shrink	Words with 'sh' (Alba Book 4)

Teaching aim: Reading practice

Teaching guidelines: Photocopy this page onto card and cut into reading cards.

Book 4: Reading and spelling

Two-syllable words with 'sh'

shell/fish	✓	_ _ _ _ _/_ _ _ _	
egg/shell		_ _ _/_ _ _ _ _	
ship/ment		_ _ _ _/_ _ _ _ _	
rubb/ish		_ _ _ _ _/_ _ _	
pol/ish		_ _ _/_ _ _	
fin/ish		_ _ _/_ _ _	
Brit/ish		_ _ _ _ _/_ _ _	
rad/ish		_ _ _/_ _ _	
flag/ship		_ _ _ _ _/_ _ _ _	

Teaching aims: Reading and spelling words with 'sh'.

Teaching guidelines: Fold this sheet along the dotted line. Ask the pupil to read the words on the left and tick the words she/he has read correctly. Ask the pupil to turn over the sheet and dictate the words to the pupil. Ask the pupil to spell the words by segmenting and sounding out the sounds as she/he writes them on the lines. Ask the pupil to open the sheet and tick the words she/he has spelled correctly.

Book 4: Reading practice

Two-syllable words with ‘ch’ and ‘sh’

finish	British	channel
ostrich	chestnut	eggshell
publish	cherub	radish
polish	chaffinch	flagship
lunchbox	attach	rubbish
sluggish	selfish	chirrup
shellfish	shipment	Two-syllable words with ‘ch’ and ‘sh’ (Alba Book 4)

Teaching aim: Reading practice

Teaching guidelines: Photocopy this page onto card and cut into reading cards.

Book 4: 4-in-a-row game 'sh'

shop	shell	shut	wish	hush
dash	brush	smash	shrug	shed
shin	ship	shall	stash	shift
shred	shot	rush	gash	shun
fish	lash	posh	flush	splash
clash	brash	shrub	fresh	crash
shelf	shrimp	shrink	crush	flash

A game for two players: Play with two sets of coloured counters. Players take turns to read a word and put a counter on it. The winner is the first to get four of his or her counters in a row in any direction. The winner places a counter on a fish symbol. The game is played four times until all the fish symbols are covered.

Book 4: Stepping stones reading game 'ch' and 'sh' words

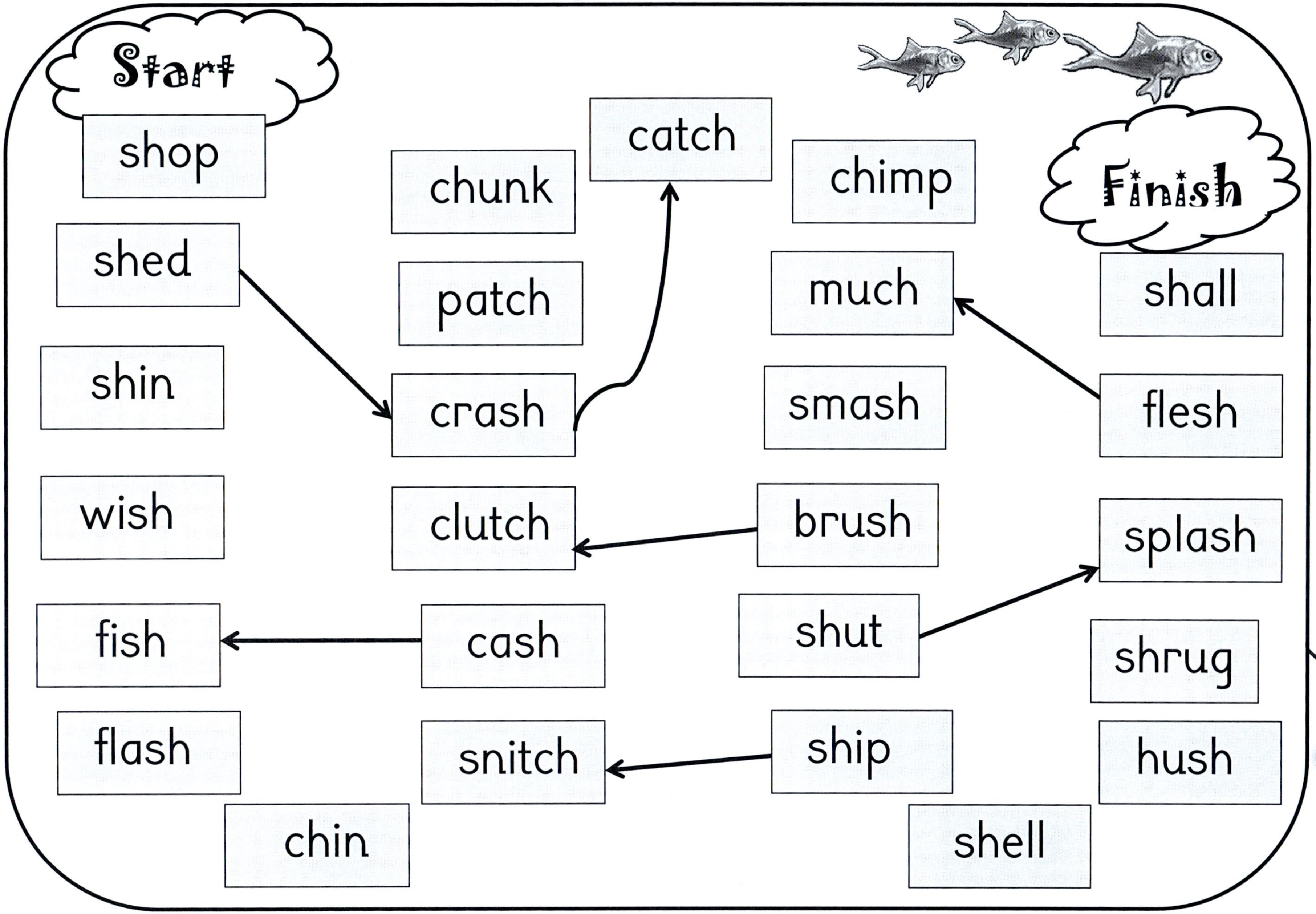

A game for 1–4 players: Play with counters and dice.
Players should read aloud the words that they land on at the end of each turn and follow the direction arrows if they land on them.

Book 4: Word-building with 'th'

th	i	n
th	*i*	*n*

Teaching aims:

- Learn the two sounds for the spelling <th>
- Segment and blend words with the spelling <th>

Teaching guidelines:

Use a white board on which three lines have been drawn. Print a card from the appendix for the spelling <th>. Add it to the cards with the letters of the alphabet from previous levels.

Teach word-building with the spelling <th>:

Teach the spelling <th>. Explain that it can represent two different sounds: 'th' as in 'thin' and 'th' as in 'this'. Select a word from the list below. Use only the letters needed to build that word and jumble them up. Ask the pupil to build that word by listening to the sounds in the words and segmenting all the sounds in the words, one at a time. The pupil then brings down each card once he/she has segmented the sound in the word. Ask the pupil to read the word he/she has built. Ask the pupil to write the word under the lines, saying the sounds as he/she writes each sound. Draw more lines for longer words.

Word list for word-building, reading and spelling:

'th' as in 'thin': thin, fifth, thrill, thank, think, moth, broth, thud, throb, froth, depth, cloth, width
'th' as in 'this': this, that, then, them, thus, with

thin	✓	___ ___ ___	
thank		___ ___ ___ ___	
think		___ ___ ___ ___	
moth		___ ___ ___	
them		___ ___ ___	
with		___ ___ ___	
this		___ ___ ___	
that		___ ___ ___	
then		___ ___ ___	

Teaching aims: Reading and spelling words with spelling <th>.

Teaching guidelines: Fold this sheet along the dotted line. Ask the pupil to read the words on the left and tick the words she/he has read correctly. Ask the pupil to turn over the sheet and dictate the words to the pupil. Ask the pupil to spell the words by segmenting and sounding out the sounds as she/he writes them on the lines. Ask the pupil to open the sheet and tick the words she/he has spelled correctly.

Book 4: Reading accuracy 'th' words

with
this
thin

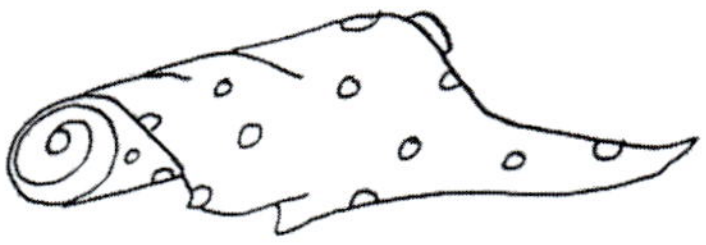

that
cloth
than

thrush
broth
throb

thank
width
think

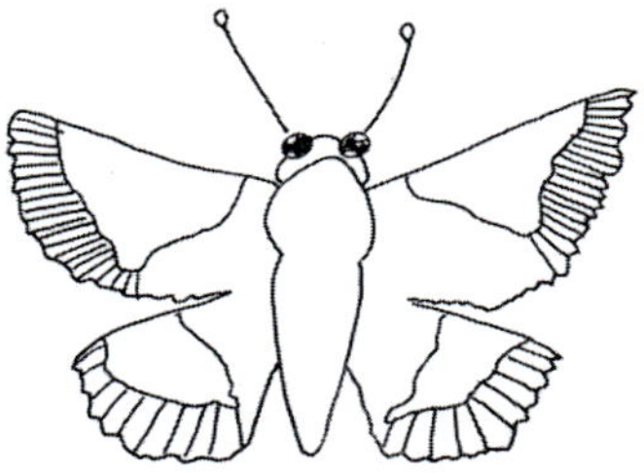

then
them
moth

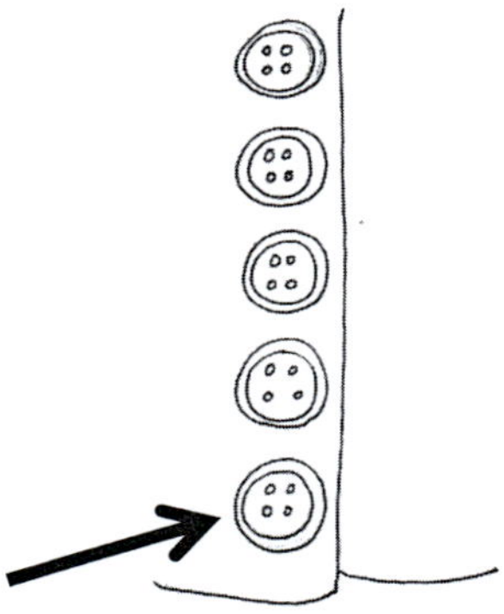

fifth
seventh
tenth

Teaching aim: Reading accuracy

Teaching guidelines: Ask the pupil to read the words in each box and circle the word that matches the picture.

this	maths	depth
then	thin	moth
thud	theft	think
broth	throb	thump
cloth	bath	that
tenth	froth	path
with	them	Words with 'th' (Alba Book 4)

Teaching aim: Reading practice

Teaching guidelines: Photocopy this page onto card and cut into reading cards.

Book 4: Reading practice

Two-syllable words with 'th'

thank ful	with held	bath ful
mamm oth	bath mat	bath tub
with in	Two-syllable words with 'th' (Syllables split) (Alba Book 4)	

	thankful	withheld
bathful	mammoth	bathmat
bathtub	within	Two-syllable words with 'th' (Alba Book 4)

Teaching aim: Reading practice

Teaching guidelines: Photocopy this page onto card and cut into reading cards. The teacher can decide whether to offer these words with the syllable split identified.

Book 4: 4-in-a-row game 'th'

that	moth	throb	maths	thin
fifth	with	thank	broth	this
them	thump	bath	froth	cloth
tenth	thud	theft	that	path
think	thrill	width	with	moth
thin	thank	then	them	broth
thrush	thud	thus	sixth	bath

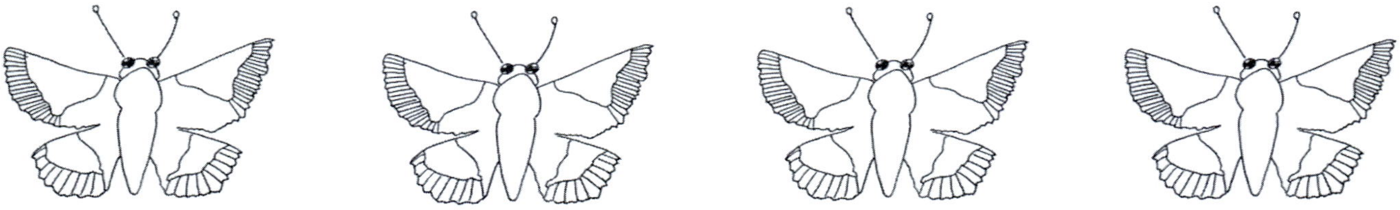

A game for two players: Play with two sets of coloured counters. Players take turns to read a word and put a counter on it. The winner is the first to get four of his or her counters in a row in any direction. The winner places a counter on a moth symbol. The game is played four times until all the moth sumbols are covered.

Book 4: Stepping stones reading game 'th' words

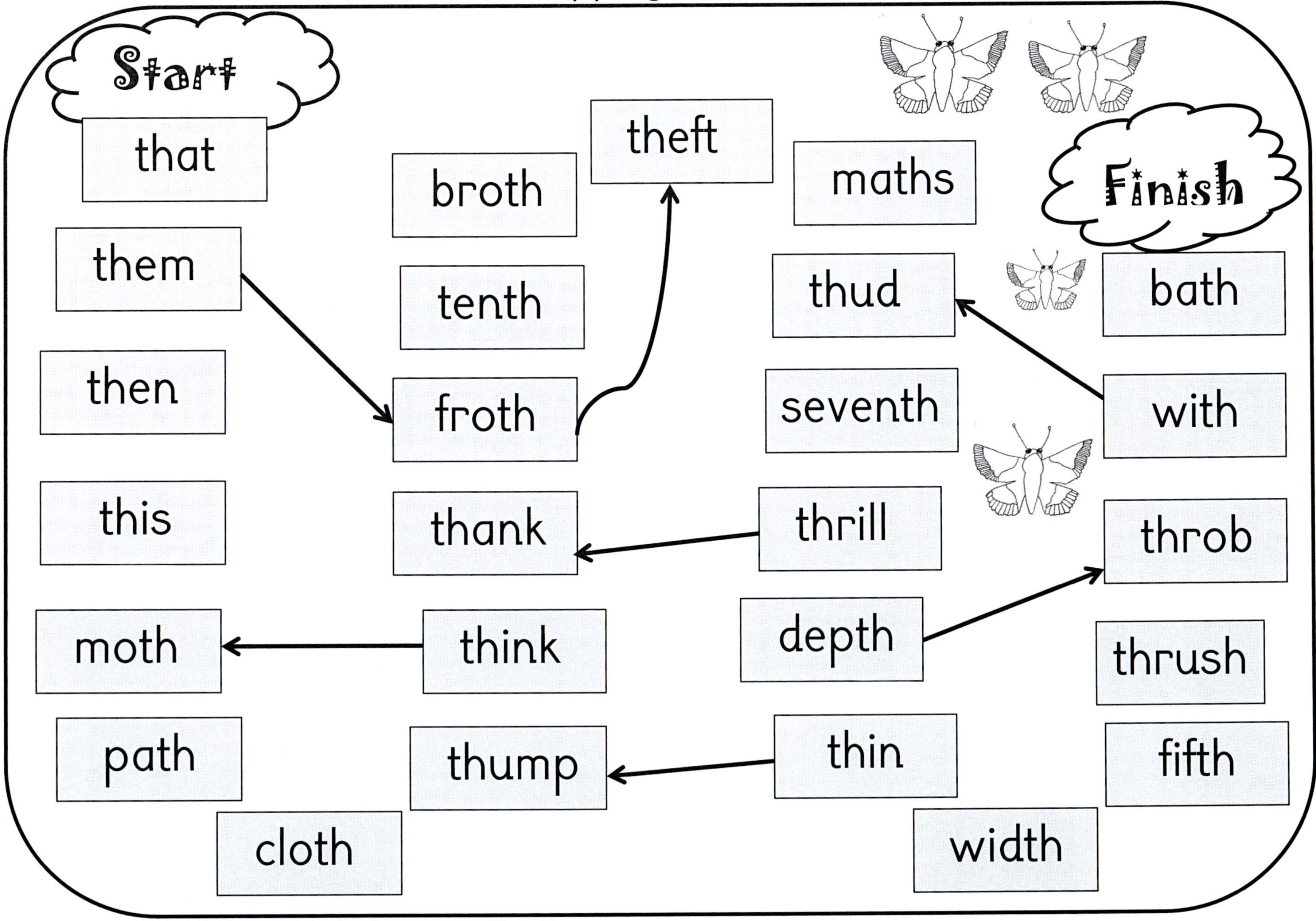

A game for 1–4 players: Play with counters and dice.
Players should read aloud the words that they land on at the end of each turn and follow the direction arrows if they land on them.

Book 4: Questions for discussion

Chapter 1

1. Why can't Alba buy lunch? (page 1)
2. What is Todd having for lunch? (page 2)

Chapter 2

1. Why does Alba inch along the bench towards Todd? (page 5)
2. What happens when the bus arrives? (page 6)

Chapter 3

1. What is making the noise that disturbs Alba? (page 8)
2. How big does the rat seem to Alba? (page 9)

Chapter 4

2. How does Alba escape from the rat? (page 11)
3. Who does Alba spot as the bus pulls away? (page 12)

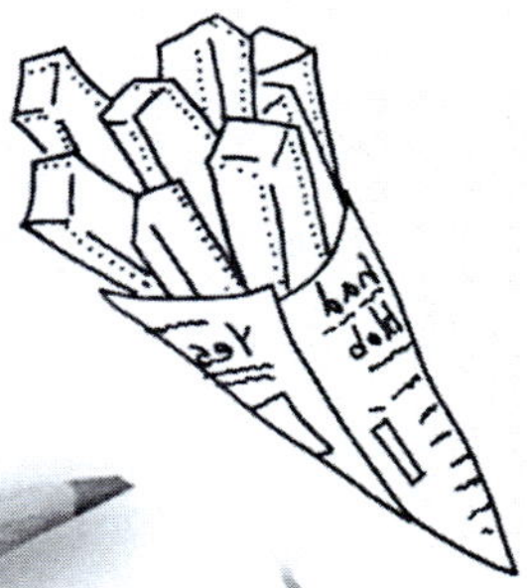

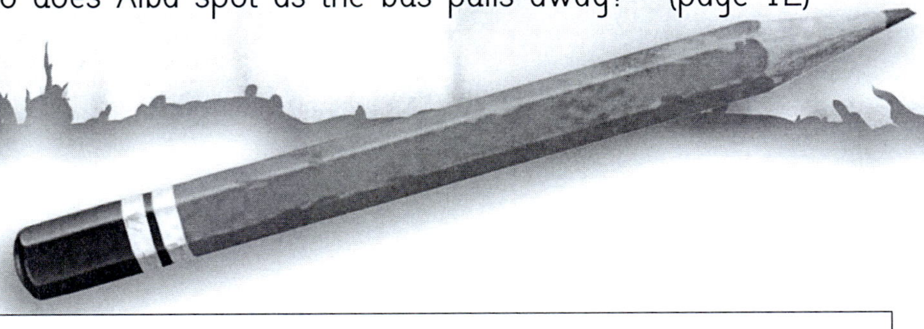

Teaching aims: Speaking and listening skills, comprehension and vocabulary.

Teaching guidelines: These questions can be discussed after reading the text.

Book 4: True or false?

	yes	no
Alba has cash to get lunch.		
Todd gets hot fish from the shop.		
Alba can smell the hot chips.		
Alba plans to pinch a hot chip.		
Todd stands at the bus stop with his chips.		
A big cat is in the bush.		
Alba runs to get on the bus.		
Max is on the bus.		

Teaching aim: Comprehension
Teaching guidelines: Ask the pupil to read the sentences and tick the boxes according to whether they are true or false.

Book 4: Picture the scene

Alba is next to a big bag of chips.

She has a chip as big as a plank in her hand.

The bag with the last pip is next to her.

A rat can smell the chips!

Teaching aims: Following instructions, comprehension and vocabulary

Teaching guidelines: Encourage the pupil to read the text carefully and draw the details of the picture as described in the text.

Book 4: Alba's diary

For lunch, I had a chip as big as a plank. I had to smash it with my hand. A rat smelt the chips! In the end, I ran to get on a bus and let the rat finish the chips.

For _ _ _ _, I _ _ _ a

_ _ _ _ _ _ _ _ _ _ a

_ _ _ _ _.

I _ _ _ to _ _ _ _ _ _

_ _ _ my _ _ _ _. A

_ _ _ _ _ _ _ _ the

_ _ _ _! _ _

the _ _ _, I _ _ _ to

_ _ _ _ _ a _ _ _ and

_ _ _ the _ _ _

_ _ _ _ _ the _ _ _ _.

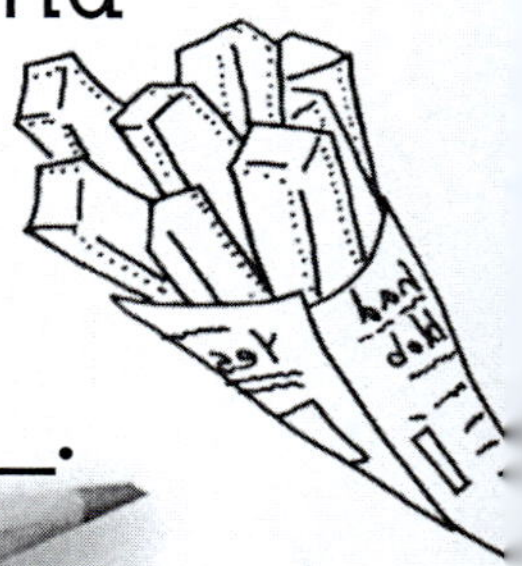

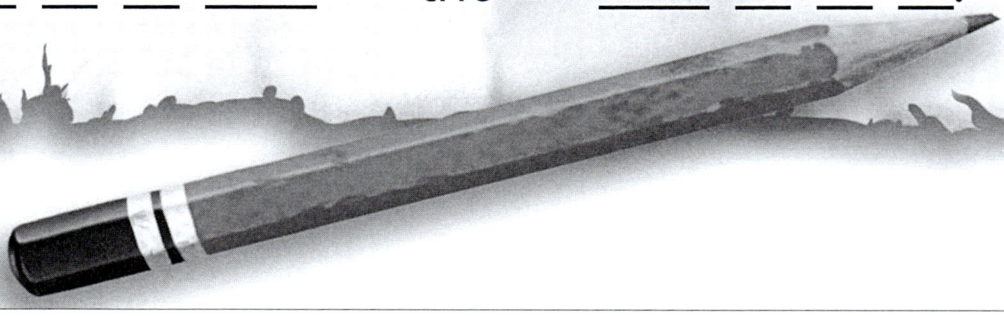

Teaching aims: Reading and spelling activity
Teaching guidelines: Encourage the pupil to copy the text at the top and insert it into the cloze exercise below it. Pupils should write a sound on each line e.g.: ch i p This activity can also be used for dictation.

Book 4: New words

New words in Book 4

hunched – sitting in a bent position
inches – moves gradually, in small stages
vanish – to disappear from sight
stinks – has a strong and offensive smell
dashes – rushes

REMINDER – A sentence **begins** with a capital letter and **ends** with a full stop.

Alba sits hunched	the bench.

The bus is still at the stop	help Alba vanish.

The rat is filthy	next to a shrub.

Alba inches along	and Alba dashes to catch it.

A spell would	and it stinks.

Teaching aims: This activity includes new vocabulary introduced in Book 4. It encourages the pupil to think about the meaning of the new words and to use them to construct a complete sentence.
Teaching guidelines: Cut the sentences into strips and cut along the centre line. Ask the pupil to match the two parts of the sentence so that they make sense. The pupil may need a reminder of what the words mean.

Book 4: Postcard home

Dear Mum,

First

Then

In the end

Love from Alba xx

Teaching aims: Comprehension and free writing

Teaching guidelines: Encourage the pupil to write about what happened in Book 4. The sentence starters provide useful cues for breaking the story into sections. Useful words are provided at the bottom of the page. The teacher can decide whether or not to offer these.

Useful words: cash lunch chips shop dash rat bus

Capital letters and full stops

REMINDER – A sentence **begins** with a capital letter and **ends** with a full stop.

alba has to get lunch she has no cash a hot lunch is just a wish

todd has a big bag of hot chips the smell of the chips drifts in the wind a big rat smells the chips

the rat runs to get the chips alba lets the rat finish the chips the bus is still at the stop alba jumps on it

Book 5: A Bit of Luck

Phonic focus: 'ck' 'ng' 'qu' 'wh' 'le' –ed **Spellings:** ck ng qu wh le ed

Contents

Book 5: Word–building 'ck' words

l	u	ck
l	u	ck

Teaching aims:

- learn the spelling alternative <ck> for the sound 'k'
- be able to segment and blend words with 'ck'

Teaching guidelines:
Use a white board on which three lines have been drawn. Print a card from the appendix for the spelling <ck>. Add it to the cards with the letters of the alphabet from previous levels.

Teach word–building with the spelling <ck>:
Select a word from the list below. Use only the letters needed to build that word and jumble them up. Ask the pupil to build that word by listening to the sounds in the words and segmenting all the sounds in the words, one at a time. The pupil then brings down each card once he/she has segmented the sound in the word. Ask the pupil to read the word he/she has built. Ask the pupil to write the word under the lines, saying the sounds as he/she writes each sound. Draw more lines for longer words.

Teaching points:

1. Ask the pupil where the <ck> spelling appears in the word (end of word).
2. Ask the pupil if he/she knows other spellings for the sound 'k' (the letters c and k).

Word list for word–building, reading and spelling:
luck, sick, pack, back, peck, rock, suck, lick, kick, tick, lock, duck, chick, shock, muck, neck, check, shack, stick, slick, thick, trick, truck, black, smack, stack, pluck, track, click, flock, stuck

Book 5: Reading and spelling 'ck' words

luck	✓	___ ___ _____	
check		_____ ___ _____	
rack		___ ___ _____	
lock		___ ___ _____	
pick		___ ___ _____	
shack		_____ ___ _____	
trick		___ ___ ___ _____	
block		___ ___ ___ _____	
stuck		___ ___ ___ _____	

Teaching aims: Reading and spelling words with spelling <ck>.

Teaching guidelines: Fold this sheet along the dotted line. Ask the pupil to read the words on the left and tick the words she/he has read correctly. Ask the pupil to turn over the sheet and dictate the words to the pupil. Ask the pupil to spell the words by segmenting and sounding out the sounds as she/he writes them on the lines. Ask the pupil to open the sheet and tick the words she/he has spelled correctly.

Book 5: Reading accuracy 'ck' words

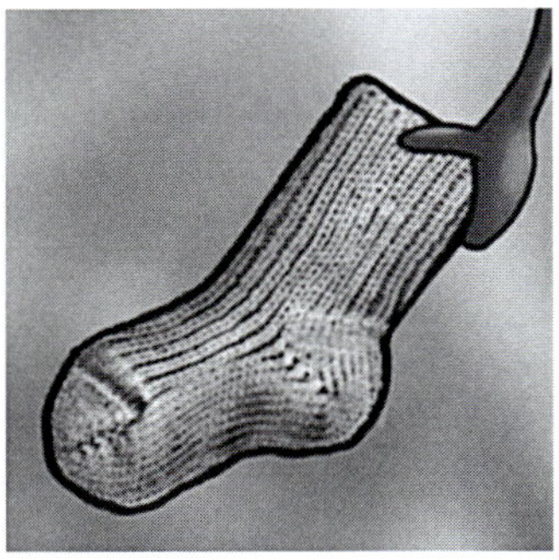

sock
suck
sick

frock
flock
clock

brick
black
back

duck
buck
black

block
rock
black

chick
chuck
check

Teaching aim: Reading accuracy

Teaching guidelines: Ask the pupil to read the words in each box and circle the word that matches the picture.

Book 5: Reading practice 'ck' words

chick	pack	lock
muck	deck	stick
speck	smock	slack
stuck	track	block
black	fleck	trick
flock	pluck	snack
clock	struck	words with 'ck' (Alba Book 5)

Teaching aim: Reading practice

Teaching guidelines: Photocopy this page onto card and cut into reading cards.

Book 5: Reading and spelling

Two-syllable words with 'ck'

back/rest	✓	_ _ _ _/_ _ _ _	
ruck/sack		_ _ _ _/_ _ _ _	
pad/lock		_ _ _/_ _ _ _	
un/stuck		_ _/_ _ _ _ _	
chop/stick		_ _ _ _/_ _ _ _ _	
pack/et		_ _ _ _/_ _	
crick/et		_ _ _ _ _/_ _	
jack/pot		_ _ _ _/_ _ _	
dip/stick		_ _ _/_ _ _ _ _	

Teaching aims: Reading and spelling words with the spelling <ck>.

Teaching guidelines: Fold this sheet along the dotted line. Ask the pupil to read the words on the left and tick the words she/he has read correctly. Ask the pupil to turn over the sheet and dictate the words to the pupil. Ask the pupil to spell the words by segmenting and sounding out the sounds as she/he writes them on the lines. Ask the pupil to open the sheet and tick the words she/he has spelled correctly.

Book 5: Reading practice

Two-syllable words with 'ck'

backrest	rucksack	padlock
unstuck	chopstick	bucket
cricket	jackpot	chopstick
stocking	backpack	unpack
chicken	duckling	stacking
tracking	backflip	jacket
pocket	attack	Two-syllable words with 'ck' (Alba Book 5)

Teaching aim: Reading practice

Teaching guidelines: Photocopy this page onto card and cut into reading cards.

Book 5: 4-in-a-row game 'ck'

luck	sick	back	pack	peck
rock	suck	lick	kick	tick
lock	duck	chick	shock	muck
neck	check	shack	stick	slick
thick	trick	truck	black	sack
stuck	stack	pluck	track	click
flock	crack	neck	brick	mock

A game for two players: Play with two sets of coloured counters. Players take turns to read a word and put a counter on it. The winner is the first to get four of his or her counters in a row in any direction. The winner places a counter on a clock symbol. The game is played four times until all the clock symbols are covered.

Book 5: Word-building 'ng' words

s	i	ng
s	*i*	*ng*

Teaching aims:

- learn the sound 'ng' and the corresponding spelling <ng>
- segment and blend words with 'ng'

Teaching guidelines:
Use a white board on which three lines have been drawn. Print a card from the appendix for the spelling <ng>. Add it to the cards with the letters of the alphabet from previous levels.

Teach word-building with the spelling <ng>:
Select a word from the list below. Use only the letters needed to build that word and jumble them up. Ask the pupil to build that word by listening to the sounds in the words and segmenting all the sounds in the words, one at a time. The pupil then brings down each card once he/she has segmented the sound in the word. Ask the pupil to read the word he/she has built. Ask the pupil to write the word under the lines, saying the sounds as he/she writes each sound. Draw more lines for longer words.

Word list for word-building, reading and spelling:
sing, fang, long, ring, bang, pang, song, gong, king, lung, thing, gang, hang, dung, rang, wing, sling, bring, sting, cling, slang, swing, fling, clang, stung, strong, prong, twang, string,

Book 5: Reading and spelling 'ng' words

sing	✓	__ __ ____	
bang		__ __ ____	
long		__ __ ____	
wing		__ __ ____	
hung		__ __ ____	
slang		__ __ __ ____	
bring		__ __ __ ____	
sting		__ __ __ ____	
strong		__ __ __ __ ____	

Teaching aims: Reading and spelling words with spelling <ng>.

Teaching guidelines: Fold this sheet along the dotted line. Ask the pupil to read the words on the left and tick the words she/he has read correctly. Ask the pupil to turn over the sheet and dictate the words to the pupil. Ask the pupil to spell the words by segmenting and sounding out the sounds as she/he writes them on the lines. Ask the pupil to open the sheet and tick the words she/he has spelled correctly.

Book 5: Reading accuracy 'ng' words

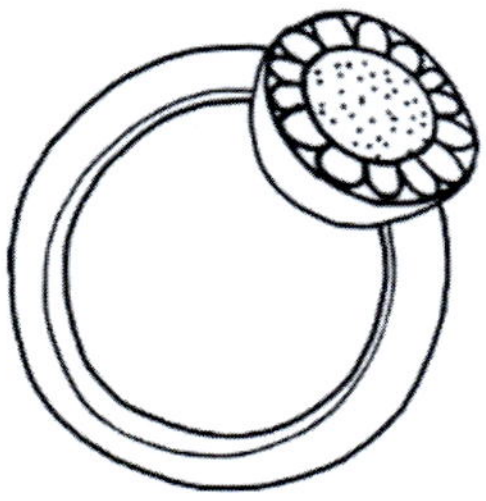

ring
bring
song

sting
king
swing

sling
sting
sing

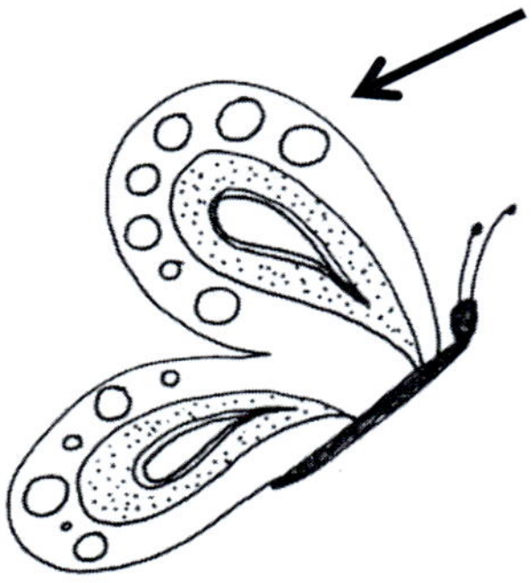

wing
ring
sing

fling
cling
bring

hang
twang
string

Teaching aim: Reading accuracy

Teaching guidelines: Ask the pupil to read the words in each box and circle the word that matches the picture.

Book 5: Reading practice 'ng' words

song	hang	ring
bang	king	lung
dung	strong	sang
wing	prong	stung
sling	fling	spring
clung	string	swing
thing	bring	words with 'ng' (Alba Book 5)

Teaching aim: Reading practice

Teaching guidelines: Photocopy this page onto card and cut into reading cards.

Book 5: Reading and spelling

Two-syllable words with ‘ng’

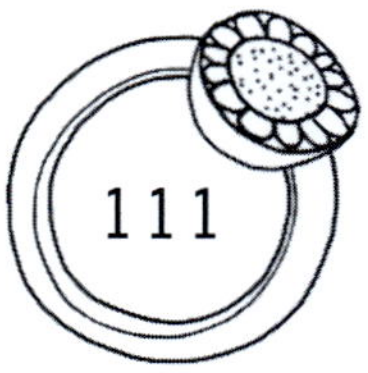

sing/song	✓	_ _ __/_ _ __	
ob/long		_ _/_ _ __	
a/long		_/_ _ __	
be/long		_ _/_ _ __	
king/dom		_ _ __/_ _ _	
think/ing		__ _ _ _/_ __	
match/ing		_ _ __ _/_ __	
rush/ing		_ _ __/_ __	
stick/ing		_ _ _ _ __/_ __	

Teaching aims: Reading and spelling words with ‘ng’.

Teaching guidelines: Fold this sheet along the dotted line. Ask the pupil to read the words on the left and tick the words she/he has read correctly. Ask the pupil to turn over the sheet and dictate the words to the pupil. Ask the pupil to spell the words by segmenting and sounding out the sounds as she/he writes them on the lines. Ask the pupil to open the sheet and tick the words she/he has spelled correctly.

Book 5: Reading practice

Two-syllable words with 'ng'

singsong	oblong	along
belong	kingdom	thinking
matching	rushing	sticking
stocking	jumping	melting
flashing	stamping	wishing
tracking	mending	funding
rocking	ticking	Two-syllable words with 'ng' (Alba Book 5)

Teaching aim: Reading practice

Teaching guidelines: Photocopy this page onto card and cut into reading cards.

Book 5: 4–in–a–row game 'ng'

ring	bring	string	sting	swing
gang	fang	gong	strong	bung
cling	fling	hang	king	wing
bang	pang	long	sing	ping
dung	thing	hung	rang	clung
stung	strong	song	wing	lung
strung	prong	thing	dong	flung

A game for two players: Play with two sets of coloured counters. Players take turns to read a word and put a counter on it. The winner is the first to get four of his or her counters in a row in any direction. The winner places a counter on a ball of string. The game is played four times until all the balls of string are covered.

Book 5: Word-building 'wh' words

wh	e	n
wh	*e*	*n*

Teaching aims:

- learn the alternative spelling <wh> for the sound 'w'
- segment and blend words with <wh>

Teaching guidelines:
Use a white board on which three lines have been drawn. Print a card from the appendix for the spelling <wh>. Add it to the cards with the letters of the alphabet from previous levels.

Teach word-building with the spelling <wh>:
Select a word from the list below. Use only the letters needed to build that word and jumble them up. Ask the pupil to build that word by listening to the sounds in the words and segmenting all the sounds in the words, one at a time. The pupil then brings down each card once he/she has segmented the sound in the word. Ask the pupil to read the word he/she has built. Ask the pupil to write the word under the lines, saying the sounds as he/she writes each sound. Draw more lines for longer words.

Word list for word-building, reading and spelling:
when, which, whip, whack, whim, whisk, whiff, whelk, whet, whiz

Book 5: Reading and spelling <wh> words

when	✓	___ ___ ___	
which		___ ___ ___	
whip		___ ___ ___	
whack		___ ___ ___	
whim		___ ___ ___	
whiff		___ ___ ___	
whiz		___ ___ ___	
whisk		___ ___ ___ ___	
whelk		___ ___ ___ ___	

Teaching aims: Reading and spelling words with the spelling <wh>.

Teaching guidelines: Fold this sheet along the dotted line. Ask the pupil to read the words on the left and tick the words she/he has read correctly. Ask the pupil to turn over the sheet and dictate the words to the pupil. Ask the pupil to spell the words by segmenting and sounding out the sounds as she/he writes them on the lines. Ask the pupil to open the sheet and tick the words she/he has spelled correctly.

Book 5: Question words card game

Switch

Switch

How?

Which?

Why?

Where?

When?

What?

Who?

Photocopy the page onto card four times, laminate and cut out. Players take turns. First player puts down a card, reading the word. Next player must play same card if he/she has one, otherwise he/she can play a switch card, and name the next word. If a player does not have a switch card and cannot follow suit, he/she misses a turn. The first player to finish all his/her cards is the winner.

when	which	whiff
wham	whack	whelk
whim	whip	whisk
whit	whop	whiz
whelks	whelp	whacking
Whitsun	whittle	whippet
whisking	whipping	words with 'wh' (Alba Book 5)

Teaching aim: Reading practice

Teaching guidelines: Photocopy this page onto card and cut into reading cards.

Book 5: Story plan with <wh> questions

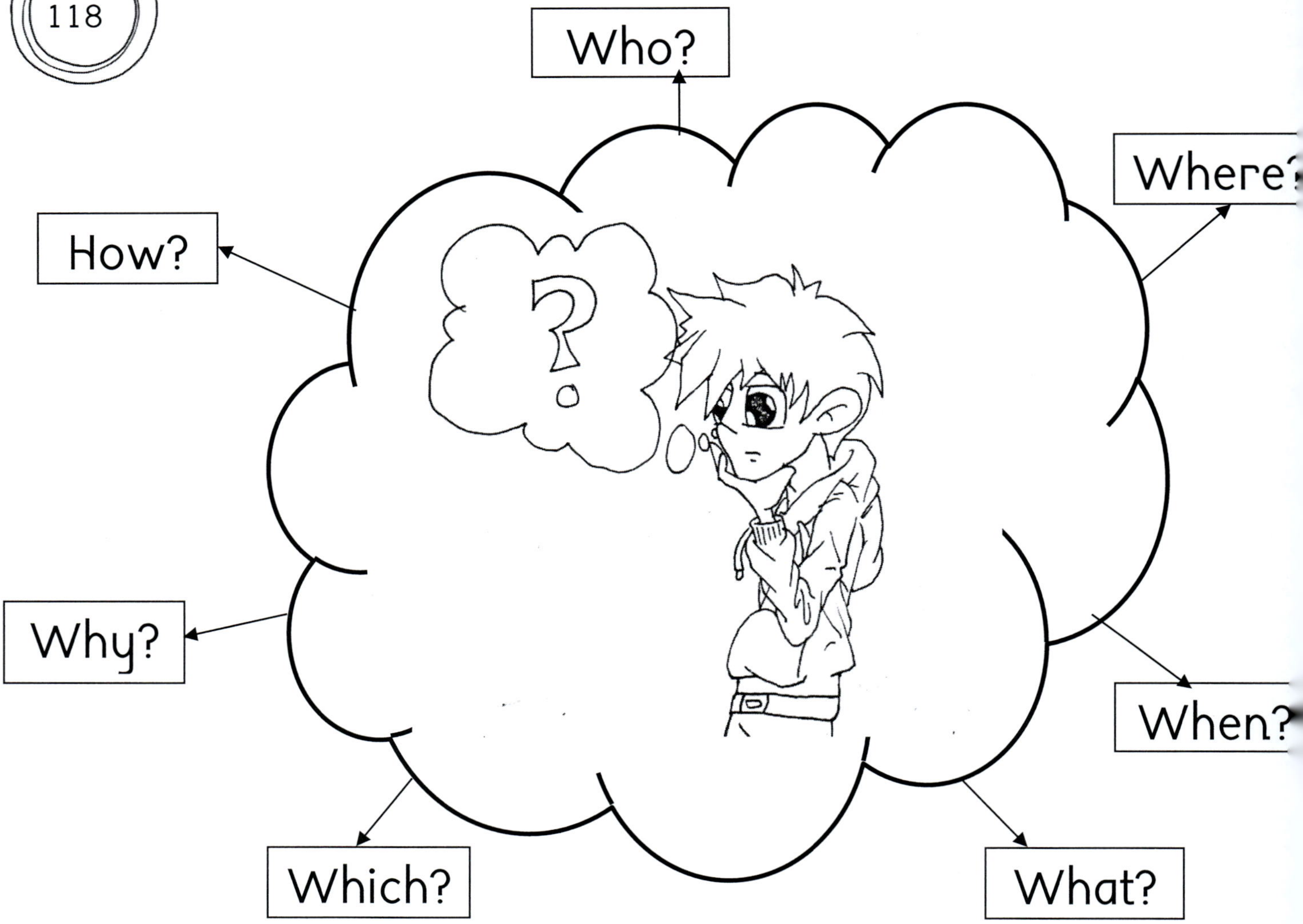

Title:

Who? ______________________________

Where? ______________________________

When? ______________________________

What? ______________________________

Which? ______________________________

Why? ______________________________

Teaching guidelines: Encourage the pupil to use this sheet to help with planning for creative writing.

Book 5: Word-building ‘qu’ words

qu	i	z
qu	*i*	*z*

Note: The sound of the letter <q> is ‘k’ as in the word ‘Iraq’. As this spelling is uncommon, the more common combination of the letters <qu> are taught as in the words: quick, queen etc. This common spelling represents two sounds – ‘kw’.

Teaching aims:

- learn the sounds and spelling of <qu>
- segment and blend words with <qu>

Teaching guidelines:
Use a white board on which three lines have been drawn. Print a card from the appendix for the spelling <qu>. Add it to the cards with the letters of the alphabet from previous levels.

Teach word-building with the spelling <qu>:
Select a word from the list below. Use only the letters needed to build that word and jumble them up. Ask the pupil to build that word by listening to the sounds in the words and segmenting all the sounds in the words, one at a time. The pupil then brings down each card once he/she has segmented the sound in the word. Ask the pupil to read the word he/she has built. Ask the pupil to write the word under the lines, saying the sounds as he/she writes each sound. Draw more lines for longer words.

Word list for word-building, reading and spelling:
quit, quick, quid, quack, quest, quiff, quill, quiz, squid, quench, quilt, squint, squib

Book 5: Reading and spelling <qu> words

quit	✓	___ ___ ___	
quack		___ ___ ___	
quiz		___ ___ ___	
quiff		___ ___ ___	
quid		___ ___ ___	
quilt		___ ___ ___ ___	
quest		___ ___ ___ ___	
squid		___ ___ ___ ___	
quench		___ ___ ___ ___	

Teaching aims: Reading and spelling words with the spelling <qu>.

Teaching guidelines: Fold this sheet along the dotted line. Ask the pupil to read the words on the left and tick the words she/he has read correctly. Ask the pupil to turn over the sheet and dictate the words to the pupil. Ask the pupil to spell the words by segmenting and sounding out the sounds as she/he writes them on the lines. Ask the pupil to open the sheet and tick the words she/he has spelled correctly.

Book 5: 4-in-a-row game ‘wh’

when	which	whip	whack	whim
quit	quick	quest	quack	quiz
whisk	whiff	whelk	whiz	whittle
quiff	squid	quell	quill	quest
when	which	whelp	whacks	whims
equip	quench	quip	squib	quins
wham	whit	whelks	whizz	when

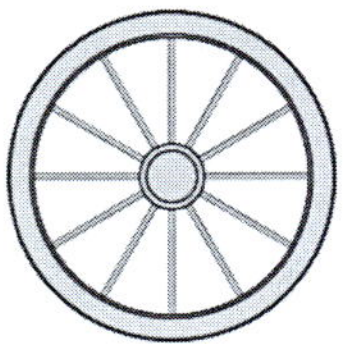
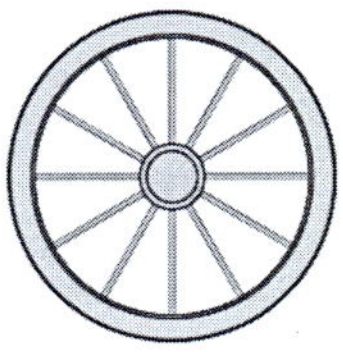

A game for two players: Play with two sets of coloured counters. Players take turns to read a word and put a counter on it. The winner is the first to get four of his or her counters in a row in any direction. The winner places a counter on a wheel. The game is played four times until all the wheels are covered.

Book 5: Reading practice <qu> words

quit	quick	quest
quip	quits	quill
quell	quin	quack
quilt	quid	quiz
quiff	squid	squelch
squib	squint	squish
quitting	request	Words with 'qu' (Alba Book 5)

Teaching aim: Reading practice

Teaching guidelines: Photocopy this page onto card and cut into reading cards.

Book 5: Word-building 'le' words

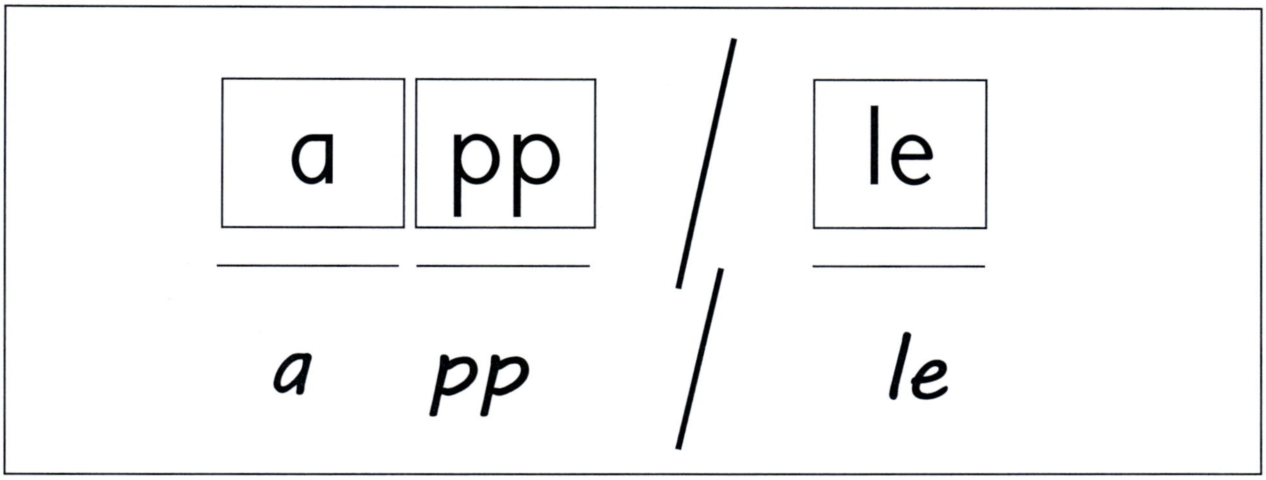

Teaching aims:

- learn the alternative spelling <le> for the sound 'l'
- blend and segment multisyllable words with the spelling <le>

Teaching guidelines:

Draw the number of lines for the sounds within each syllable and a slash between the syllables.

Make or print cards from the appendix for the spelling <le> and the cards with two letters for the sounds <p>, <b>, <t> and <d>.

Teach word-building with <le> ending:

Select a word from the word list below. Use only the letters needed to build that word and jumble them up. Ask the pupil to build the first syllable in the word by listening to the sounds in the syllable and segmenting all the sounds in the syllable, one at a time. The pupil then brings down each card once he/she has segmented the sound in the word. Ask the pupil to read the syllable he/she has built. Repeat the steps with the second syllable. Ask the pupil to read the word first in two separate syllables and then as one word. Ask the pupil to write the word under the lines, saying the sounds within the syllables as he/she writes each sound; and then to reread the word.

Teaching point:

One can also split the word 'a /pp le'.

Word list for word-building, reading and spelling:

apple, pebble, fiddle, gobble, muddle, gabble, settle, middle, doddle, muffle, saddle, kettle, little, gamble, simple, single, handle, temple, mantle, candle, dimple, ramble, bramble, stumble

Book 5: Reading and spelling 'le' words

app le	✓	____/___	
pudd le		_____/___	
midd le		_____/___	
bott le		_____/___	
litt le		_____/___	
gobb le		_____/___	
simp le		_____/___	
hand le		_____/___	
sing le		_____/___	

Teaching aims: Reading and spelling words ending with the spelling <le>.

Teaching guidelines: Fold this sheet along the dotted line. Ask the pupil to read the words on the left and tick the words she/he has read correctly. Ask the pupil to turn over the sheet and dictate the words to the pupil. Ask the pupil to spell the words by segmenting and sounding out the sounds as she/he writes them on the lines. Ask the pupil to open the sheet and tick the words she/he has spelled correctly.

Book 5: Reading practice 'le' words

nettle	snuggle	raffle
wobble	apple	middle
heckle	bottle	drizzle
snuffle	angle	temple
thimble	toggle	tumble
bramble	dwindle	uncle
shingle	chuckle	words with 'le' (Alba Book 5)

Teaching aim: Reading practice

Teaching guidelines: Photocopy this page onto card and cut into reading cards.

Book 5: Stepping stones reading game 'le' words

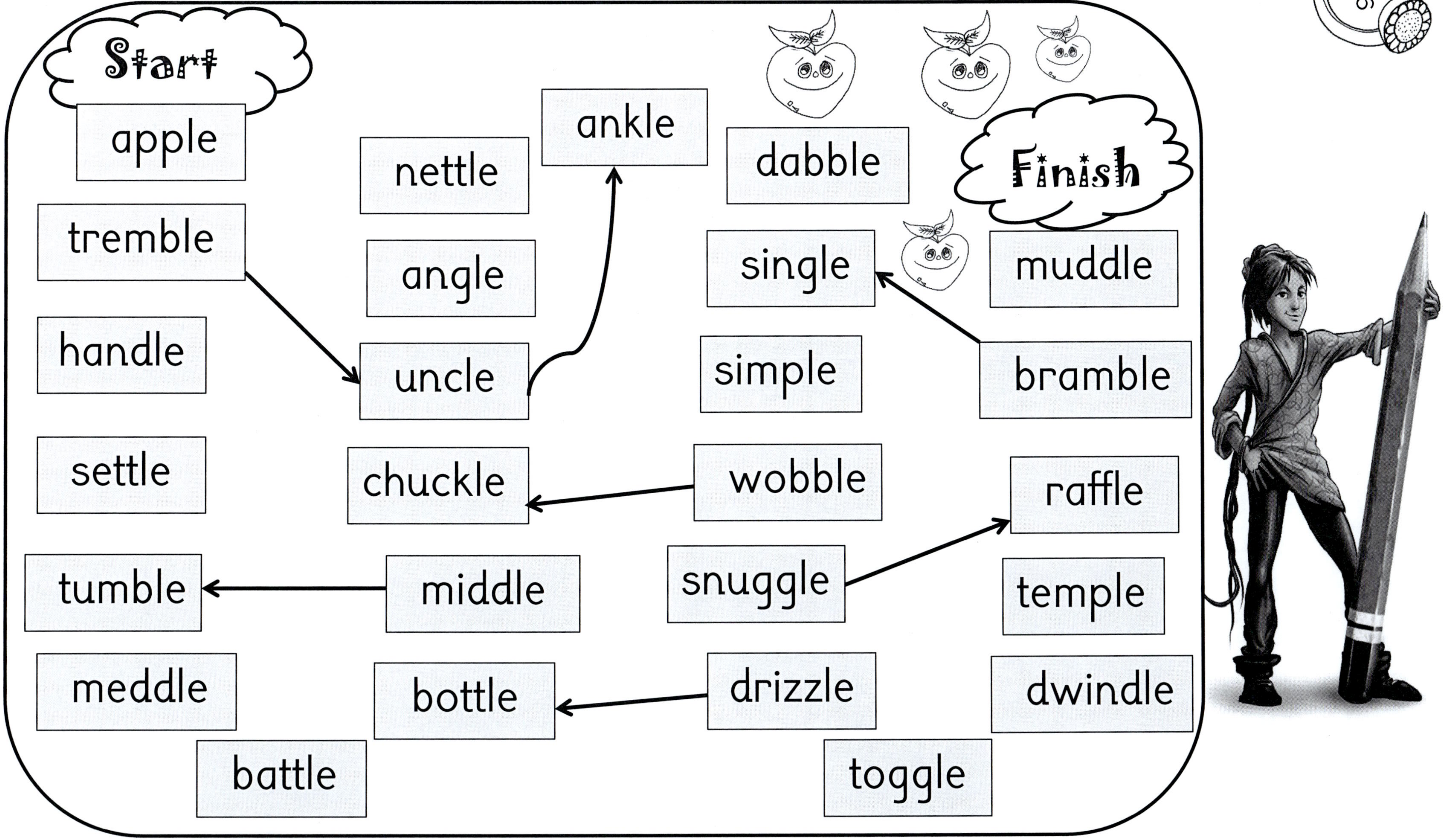

A game for 1–4 players: Play with counters and dice.
Players should read aloud the words that they land on at the end of each turn and follow the direction arrows if they land on them.

Book 5: The three sounds of '–ed'

t	d	id

skipped	jumped	tripped
landed	hugged	spotted
rubbed	panted	scanned
puffed	yelled	lifted
snapped	skidded	grabbed

Teaching guidelines: This can be used as a sorting game or as a written exercise. First, discuss verbs in the past, present and future tenses and explain that –ed is an ending for the past tense. Ask the pupil to listen carefully to the sound of –ed at the end of each word and write the word in the correct column. This will help the pupil with spelling.

To make a game, photocopy this sheet onto card to make one card for each player. Place the word cards upside down in a pile. Players take turns to pick one up. The first to have three cards in each box is the winner.

Book 5: Stepping stones reading game '–ed' words

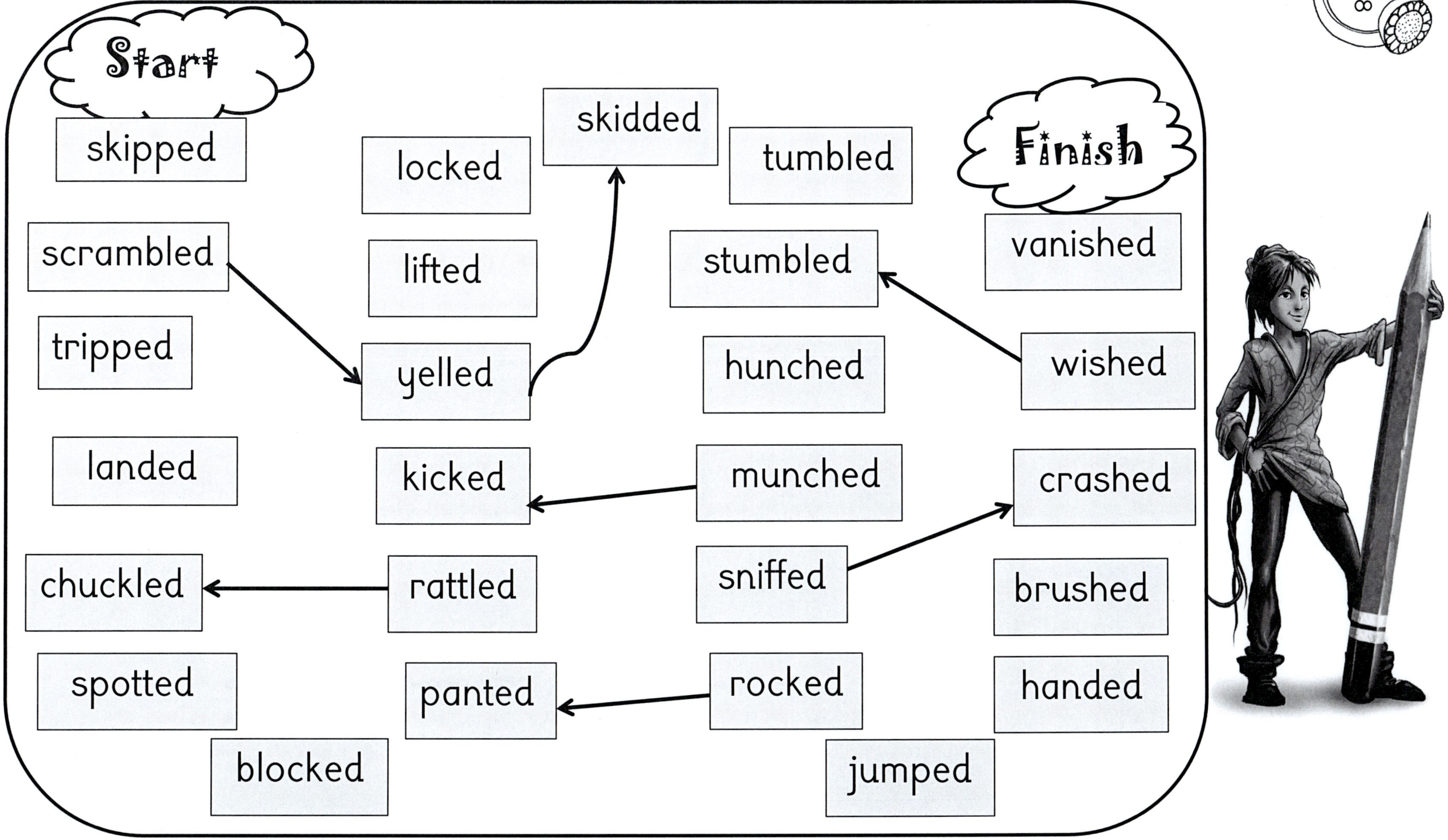

A game for 1–4 players: Play with counters and dice.
Players should read aloud the words that they land on at the end of each turn and follow the direction arrows if they land on them.

Book 5: Questions for discussion

Chapter 1

1. What happens when Alba gets on the bus? (page 1)
2. What does Alba bump into? (page 2)
3. What gives her some protection? (page 3)

Chapter 2

1. What has Todd lost? (page 4)
2. Where does Alba find it? (page 5)

Chapter 3

1. How does Alba reach Todd's lap? (page 8)
2. Where does she put the ring? (page 10)

Chapter 4

1. Where does Alba decide to rest? (page 11)
2. Does Todd realise how the ring got back in the box? (page 12)

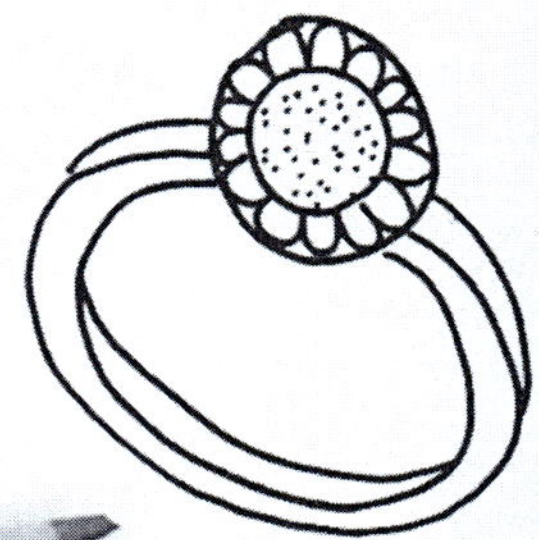

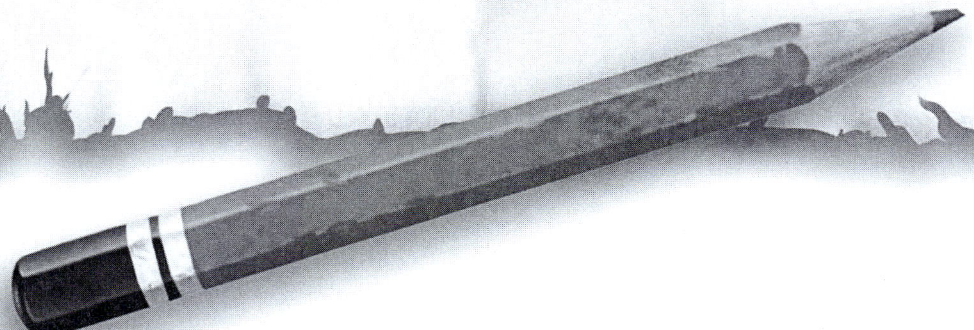

Teaching aims: Speaking and listening skills, comprehension and vocabulary.

Teaching guidelines: These questions can be discussed after reading the text

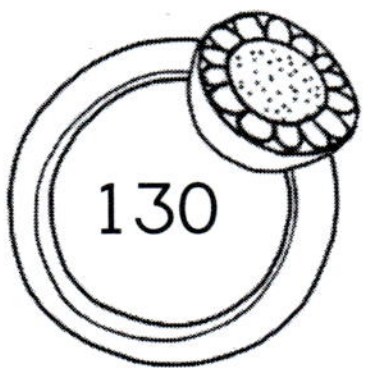

Book 5: True or false?

	yes	no
Alba clung to a soft, thick vest.	☐	☐
Alba spotted Max on the bus.	☐	☐
Todd had dropped a ring from his pocket.	☐	☐
The ring was trapped under a plastic bottle.	☐	☐
Alba swung onto Todd's lap on a long string.	☐	☐
Alba dropped the ring back in the ring box.	☐	☐
Todd did not spot that the ring was back.	☐	☐
Alba stopped to rest in Todd's pocket.	☐	☐

Teaching aim: Comprehension
Teaching guidelines: Ask the pupil to read the sentences and tick the boxes according to whether they are true or false.

Book 5: Picture the scene

Alba is holding a long string.

The ring is on her back.

She is standing on top of a bottle.

Next to the bottle is a thick sock.

Teaching aims: Following instructions, comprehension and vocabulary

Teaching guidelines: Encourage the pupil to read the text carefully and draw the details of the picture as described in the text.

Book 5: Alba's diary

I had a lift on a bus! I spotted a ring stuck in a crack. I grabbed it and slung it on my back. Todd was glad to get it back.

I ___ ___ ___ a ___ ___ ___ ___

___ ___ a ___ ___ ___! I

___ ___ ___ _____ _____ a ___ ___ _____

___ ___ ___ _____ ___ ___ a

___ ___ ___ _____. I ___ ___ ___ _____ _____

___ ___ ___ ___ ___ ___ ___ ___ _____

___ ___ ___ ___ my ___ ___ _____.

___ ___ _____ was ___ ___ ___ ___

to ___ ___ ___ ___ ___

___ ___ _____.

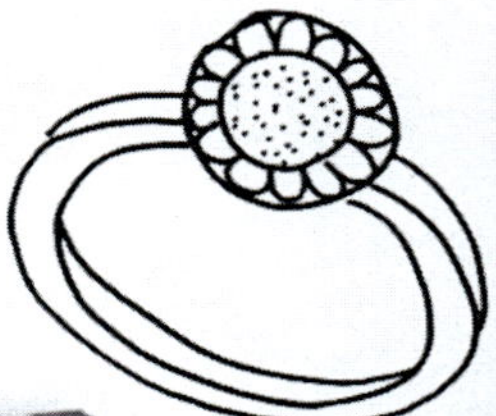

Teaching aims: Reading and spelling activity
Teaching guidelines: Encourage the pupil to copy the text at the top and insert it into the cloze exercise below it. Pupils should write a sound on each line e.g: l i f t. This activity can also be used for dictation.

Book 5: New words

New words in Book 5

tumbled – rolled end over end, as in falling.
crumpled – wrinkled or crushed
clung – held tight
slung – threw something
glum – sad and gloomy

REMINDER – A sentence **begins** with a capital letter and **ends** with a full stop.

Alba tumbled	and felt glum.

Alba clung	the ring on her back.

Crumpled bus tickets	to the back of the bus.

Alba slung	to a soft, thick sock.

Todd had lost the ring	rolled along the bus.

Teaching aims: This activity includes new vocabulary introduced in Book 5. It encourages the pupil to think about the meaning of the new words and to use them to construct a complete sentence.
Teaching guidelines: Cut the sentences into strips and cut along the centre line. Ask the pupil to match the two parts of the sentence so that they make sense. The pupil may need a reminder of what the words mean.

Book 5: Postcard home

Dear Mum,

First

Then

In the end

Love from Alba xxx

Teaching aims: Comprehension and free writing

Teaching guidelines: Encourage the pupil to write about what happened in Book 5. The sentence starters provide useful cues for breaking the story into sections. Useful words are provided at the bottom of the page. The teacher can decide whether or not to offer these.

Useful words: tumbled ring string swung pocket

Book 5: Punctuation

Capital letters and full stops

REMINDER – A sentence **begins** with a capital letter and **ends** with a full stop.

the bus rocks as it sets off alba tumbles to the back of the bus

todd has lost his ring he is glum alba spots the ring stuck in a crack

alba grabs the ring she slings it on her back she drops it into the pocket of todd's jacket

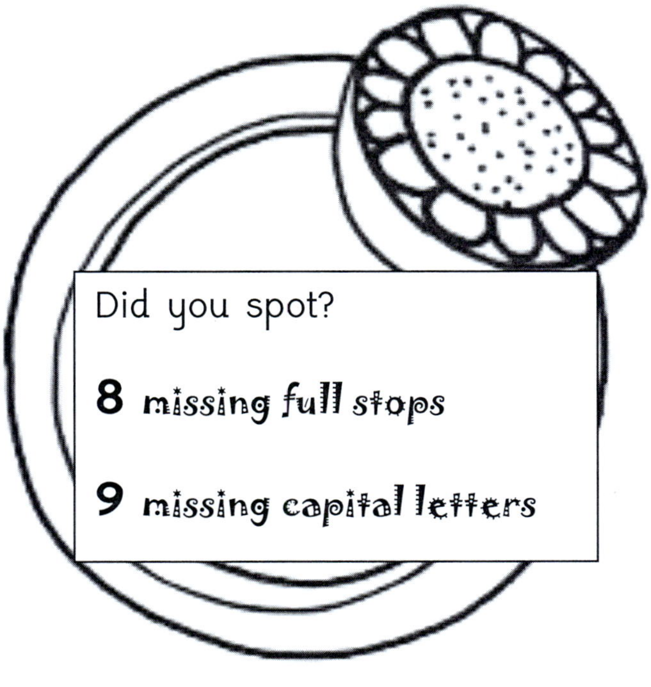

Did you spot?

8 missing full stops

9 missing capital letters

Book 6: A Brave Escape

Phonic focus: 'ae' **Spellings:** ay, ai, a and a–e

Contents

Book 6: Word-building 'ae' words

r	ai	n
r	*ai*	*n*

Teaching aims:

- learn the spelling alternatives <ai>, <ay> and <a> for the sound 'ae'
- be able to segment and blend words with these three different spellings

Teaching guidelines:

Use a white board on which three lines have been drawn. Print a card from the appendix for the spellings <ai>, <ay> and <a>. Add these to the cards with the letters of the alphabet from previous levels.

Teach word-building with the spellings <ai>, <ay> and <a>:

Select a word from the lists below. Teachers can choose whether to start work with one spelling of the sound or whether to begin with multiple spellings. Use only the letters needed to build that word and jumble them up. Ask the pupil to build that word by listening to the sounds in the words and segmenting all the sounds in the words, one at a time. The pupil then brings down each card once he/she has segmented the sound in the word. Ask the pupil to read the word he/she has built. Ask the pupil to write the word under the lines saying the sounds as he/she writes each sound. Draw more lines for longer words.

Word lists for word-building, reading and spelling:

ai	ay	a
main raid pail	day way may pay	bacon
snail paint stain	stay clay	table
strain afraid contain	stray away display	able

Book 6: Word–building 'a–e' words

c		k		
n		m		
l		t		
s		f		
f	l		m	
s	n		k	

a e	a e	a e	a e	a e	a e

Teaching aims:

- learn the spelling <a–e> for the sound 'ae'
- be able to segment and blend words with this spelling

Teaching guidelines:

Cut out the 'ae' cards. Ask the pupil to cut along the central line in the spelling cards and insert the split spelling of the 'ae' in the words above. Ask the pupil to say the sounds as they blend them into a word and then write the word on the lines, saying the sounds as they do.

Book 6: Timed reading 'a–e' words

Beat your own record!

hat	hate	man	mane	Sam	same	mad	made
dam	dame	tap	tape	fat	fate	pan	pane
nap	nape	mat	mate	van	vane	gap	gape
Dan	Dane	rat	rate	cap	cape	rag	rage

wake	name	yap	plane	flap	snag	tame	Dad	
map	damp	late	land	Jane	tag	ham	plate	
shame	stab	snake	rat	bag	lane	pale	fame	
zap	tale	man	gap	fan	cage	hat	face	jam

Teaching guidelines: Ask the pupil to read the text as fast as possible to try to beat his/her own time. Y will need a timer for this activity.

Book 6: Reading and spelling 'ae' words with <ay> and <ai> spellings

play	✓	___ ___ _____	
stay		___ ___ _____	
tray		___ ___ _____	
sway		___ ___ _____	

rain		___ _____ ___	
mail		___ _____ ___	
wait		___ _____ ___	
faint		___ _____ ___ ___	

Teaching aims: Reading and spelling 'ae' words with the spellings <ay> and <ai>.

Teaching guidelines: Fold this sheet along the dotted line. Ask the pupil to read the words on the left and tick the words she/he has read correctly. Ask the pupil to turn over the sheet and dictate the words to the pupil. Ask the pupil to spell the words by segmenting and sounding out the sounds as she/he writes them on the lines. Ask the pupil to open the sheet and tick the words she/he has spelled correctly.

Book 6: Reading and spelling 'ae' words with <a> and <a–e> spellings

bacon	✓
able	
sacred	
David	

came	
fade	
hate	
sale	

Teaching aims: Reading and spelling 'ae' words with the spellings <a> and <a–e>.

Teaching guidelines: Fold this sheet along the dotted line. Ask the pupil to read the words on the left and tick the words she/he has read correctly. Ask the pupil to turn over the sheet and dictate the words to the pupil. Ask the pupil to spell the words by segmenting and sounding out the sounds as she/he writes them on the lines. Ask the pupil to open the sheet and tick the words she/he has spelled correctly.

Book 6: Reading and sorting words with 'ae' spellings

ai	ay	a	a–e

sale	able	May	faint
shame	late	paint	tray
nail	sacred	flame	quaint
day	pain	table	mate
David	stay	trail	haze
making	drain	whale	spray
strain	blame	pray	brain
stain	frame	fade	clay

Teaching guidelines: Photocopy this page onto card and cut into reading cards. Read and sort the cards out according to the 'ae' spellings. The cards at the top of the sheet can be used as headings for each spelling. These spellings can be recorded on the following sheet.

Book 6: Spellings: 'ae'

ai

a–e

a

ay

Teaching guidelines: List the words from the reading and sorting cards according to the spelling of the sound 'ae'.

Book 6: Reading and spelling

Two-syllable words with 'ae' spellings

g**a**t**e**/crash	✓		
h**ay**/stack			
n**ai**l/brush			
b**a**/con			
bl**a**m**e**/less			
es/c**a**p**e**			
dis/pl**ay**			
con/t**ain**			
m**a**king			

Teaching aims: Reading and spelling words with alternative spellings of the sound 'ae'.

Teaching guidelines: Fold this sheet along the dotted line. Ask the pupil to read the words on the left and tick the words she/he has read correctly. Ask the pupil to turn over the sheet and dictate the words to the pupil. Ask the pupil to spell the words by segmenting and sounding out the sounds as she/he writes them on the lines. Ask the pupil to open the sheet and tick the words she/he has spelled correctly.

Book 6: Reading practice

Two-syllable words with 'ae' spellings

(syllables split)

gate crash	hay stack	pay ment
com plain	pain ful	ta ble
blame less	rail way	con tain
dis play	sta ble	lamp shade
es cape	a way	pain less
gang way	nail brush	a fraid
a wake	ma king	Two-syllable words with 'ae' spellings (syllables split) (Alba Book 6)

Teaching aim: Reading practice

Teaching guidelines: Photocopy this page onto card and cut into reading cards.

Book 6: Reading practice

Two-syllable words with 'ae' spellings

gatecrash	haystack	payment
complain	painful	table
blameless	railway	contain
display	stable	lampshade
escape	away	painless
gangway	nailbrush	afraid
awake	braking	Two-syllable words with 'ae' spellings (Alba Book 6)

Teaching aim: Reading practice

Teaching guidelines: Photocopy this page onto card and cut into reading cards.

Book 6: 4-in-a-row game 'ae'

way	gain	able	take	say
pale	fail	made	table	gaze
David	clay	fake	trail	brave
tray	paint	paid	sway	stay
faint	play	shave	waste	slave
taste	jail	trade	quail	snake
brain	date	tame	mate	pain

A game for two players: Play with two sets of coloured counters. Players take turns to read a word and put a counter on it. The winner is the first to get four of his or her counters in a row in any direction. The winner places a counter on a cake. The game is played four times until all the cakes are covered.

Book 6: Stepping stones reading game 'ae' words

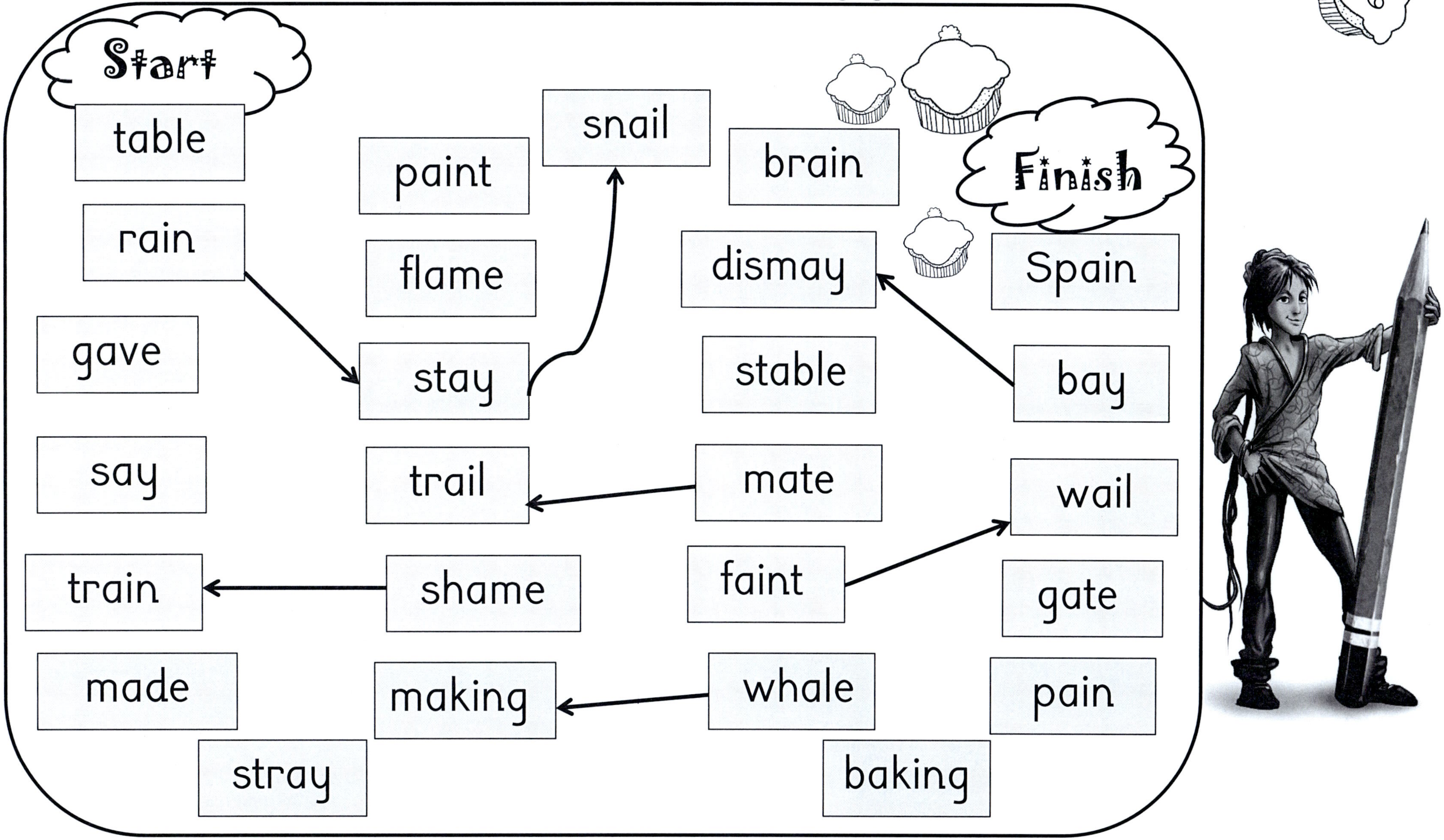

A game for 1–4 players: Play with counters and dice.
Players should read aloud the words that they land on at the end of each turn and follow the direction arrows if they land on them.

Book 6: Questions for discussion

Chapter 2

1. Where does Todd go when he gets off the bus? (page 4)
2. Why is Alba frightened? (page 4)
3. Where has Todd put his jacket? (page 4)
4. How does Alba fall off the shelf? (page 5)
5. How does she try to save herself? (page 6)

Chapter 3

1. Why do you think the baby wants to grab Alba? (page 9)
2. How does Alba escape from him? (page 9)

Chapter 4

1. Where does Mum put the spray can? (page 11)
2. Why is Alba relieved at the end of the story? (page 12)

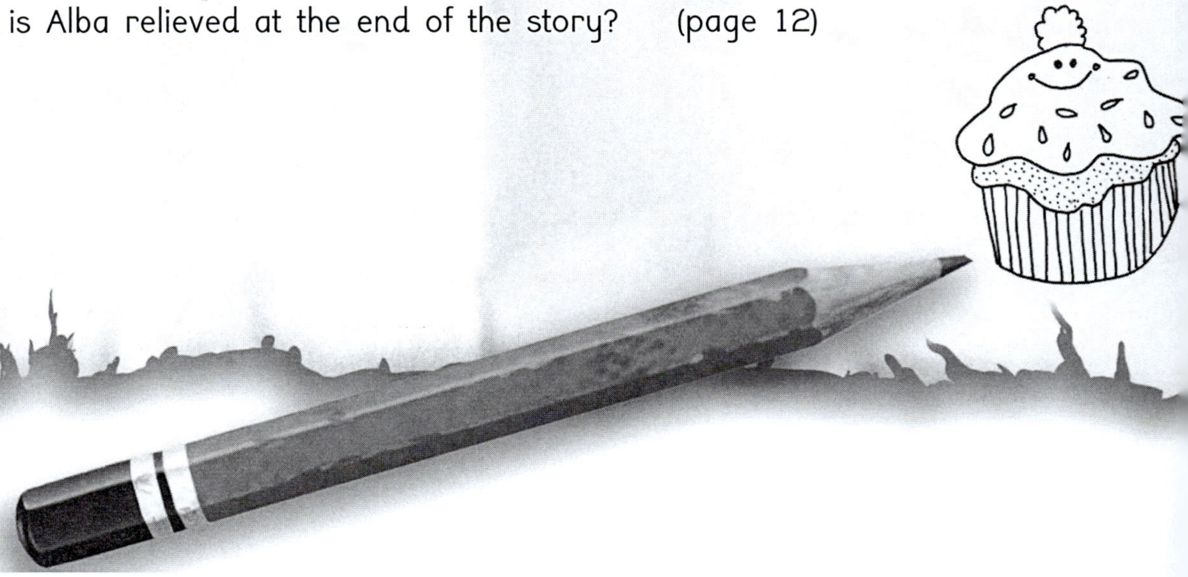

Teaching aims: Speaking and listening skills, comprehension and vocabulary.

Teaching guidelines: These questions can be discussed after reading the text.

Book 6: True or false?

	yes	no
Alba was trapped in a hot cave.		
Todd had left his jacket on the table.		
Alba bent over to smell the fresh cake.		
Alba saved herself by grabbing the table.		
The baby grabbed Alba in his fist.		
Alba jumped on a model train to escape.		
Mum sprayed Alba with milk.		
Alba left her bag and the pip in the flat.		

Teaching aim: Comprehension
Teaching guidelines: Ask the pupil to read the sentences and tick the boxes according to whether they are true or false.

Book 6: Picture the scene

The cake has 12 candles on it.

It has a big flag on top with Todd's name on it.

It has jam in the middle.

The plate has shapes on it.

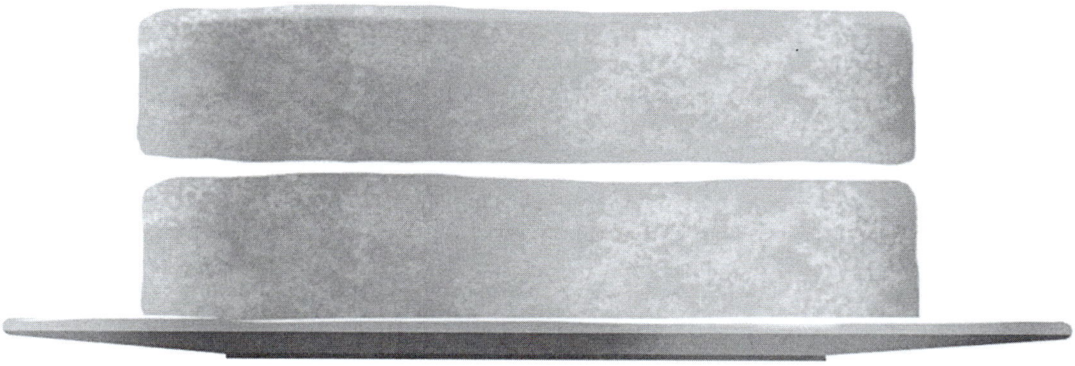

Teaching aims: Following instructions, comprehension and vocabulary

Teaching guidelines: Encourage the pupil to read the text carefully and draw the details of the picture as described in the text.

Book 6: Alba's diary

I went to Todd's flat. I had to escape from his jacket pocket. I was on a shelf a long way up. I fell off. I made my escape on a model train!

I _ _ _ _ to _ _ _ ’ _

_ _ _ _. I _ _ _ to

_ _ _ _ _ _ _ _ _ _

_ _ _ _ _ _ _ _

_ _ _ _ _. I was _ _

a _ _ _ _ a _ _ _

_ _ _ _. I _ _ _

_ _. I _ _ _ _ my

_ _ _ _ _ _ _ _ a

_ _ _ _ _ _ _ _ _ _!

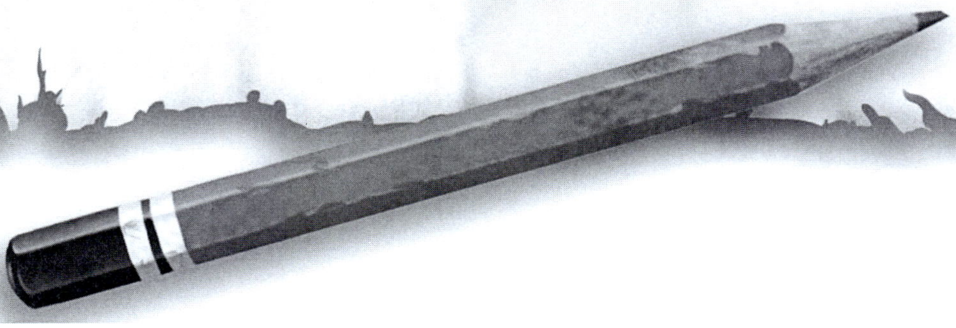

Teaching aims: Reading and spelling activity
Teaching guidelines: Encourage the pupil to copy the text at the top and insert it into the cloze exercise below it. Pupils should write a sound on each line e.g: h e l p. This activity can also be used for dictation.

Book 6: New words

New words in Book 6

strained – pushed against something with force
exclaimed – cried out suddenly
mist – a cloud of water
wailed – called out sadly or mournfully
swayed – swung to and fro

REMINDER – A sentence **begins** with a capital letter and **ends** with a full stop.

Alba strained	fell from the spray can.

A mist of soft rain	exclaimed Alba.

"The table will save me!"	against the thick cloth.

Alba swayed	grabbed at Alba.

The baby wailed and	against the table leg.

Teaching aims: This activity includes new vocabulary introduced in Book 6. It encourages the pupil to think about the meaning of the new words and to use them to construct a complete sentence.
Teaching guidelines: Cut the sentences into strips and cut along the centre line. Ask the pupil to match the two parts of the sentence so that they make sense. The pupil may need a reminder of what the words mean.

Book 6: Postcard home

Dear Mum,

First

Then

In the end

Love from Alba xxx

Teaching aims: Comprehension and free writing

Teaching guidelines: Encourage the pupil to write about what happened in Book 6. The sentence starters provide useful cues for breaking the story into sections. Useful words are provided at the bottom of the page. The teacher can decide whether or not to offer these.

Useful words: escape afraid table train baby spray

Book 6: Punctuation

Capital letters and full stops

REMINDER – A sentence **begins** with a capital letter and **ends** with a full stop.

todd went back to his flat with alba in his pocket alba was trapped in his pocket

alba was on a shelf it was a long way up and she was afraid she bent over to smell a cake and fell off the shelf

alba landed on a table a baby was amazed to see her she got away on a model train it was getting late in the day when she left the flat

Did you spot?

9 missing full stops

10 missing capital letters

Book 7: Apple Trees

Phonic focus: 'ee' **Spellings:** ee, ea, y, ey, e

Contents

Book 7: Word-building 'ee' words

l	ea	p
l	*ea*	*p*

Teaching aims:

- learn the spelling alternatives <ee>, <ea>, <e>, <y> and <ey> for the sound 'ee'
- be able to segment and blend words with these five different spellings

Teaching guidelines:

Use a white board on which three lines have been drawn. Print cards from the appendix for the spellings <ee>, <ea>, <e>, <y> and <ey>. Add these to the cards with the letters of the alphabet from previous levels.

Teachers can choose whether to start work with one spelling of the sound or whether to begin with multiple spellings.

Teach word-building with the spellings <ee>, <ea>, <e>, <y> and <ey>:

Select a word from the lists below. Use only the letters needed to build that word and jumble them up. Ask the pupil to build that word by listening to the sounds in the words and segmenting all the sounds in the words, one at a time. The pupil then brings down each card once he/she has segmented the sound in the word. Ask the pupil to read the word he/she has built. Ask the pupil to write the word under the lines, saying the sounds as he/she writes each sound. Draw more lines for longer words.

Word lists for word-building, reading and spelling:

ee	ea	e	y	ey
meet	meal	we	body	key
feed	beam	me	sadly	abbey
seem	read	he	jelly	valley
speed	cream	she	snappy	chimney

Book 7: Reading and spelling 'ee' words with <ey>, <ea> and <e> spellings

Word	Tick	Spelling	Tick
donkey	✓	__ __ __ __ ____	
trolley		__ __ __ ____ ____	
jockey		__ __ ____ ____	
team		__ ____ __	
lean		__ ____ __	
steal		__ __ ____ __	
he		__ __	
me		__ __	
she		____ __	

Teaching aims: Reading and spelling 'ee' words with the spellings <ey>,<ea> and <e>.

Teaching guidelines: Fold this sheet along the dotted line. Ask the pupil to read the words on the left and tick the words she/he has read correctly. Ask the pupil to turn over the sheet and dictate the words to the pupil. Ask the pupil to spell the words by segmenting and sounding out the sounds as she/he writes them on the lines. Ask the pupil to open the sheet and tick the words she/he has spelled correctly.

Book 7: Reading and spelling 'ee' words with <ee> and <y> spellings

meet	✓	___ ___ ___	
seem		___ ___ ___	
green		___ ___ ___ ___	
teeth		___ ___ ___	

sunny		___ ___ ___ ___	
happy		___ ___ ___ ___	
lucky		___ ___ ___ ___	
clumsy		___ ___ ___ ___ ___ ___	

Teaching aims: Reading and spelling 'ee' words with the spellings <ee> and <y>.

Teaching guidelines: Fold this sheet along the dotted line. Ask the pupil to read the words on the left and tick the words she/he has read correctly. Ask the pupil to turn over the sheet and dictate the words to the pupil. Ask the pupil to spell the words by segmenting and sounding out the sounds as she/he writes them on the lines. Ask the pupil to open the sheet and tick the words she/he has spelled correctly.

Book 7: Reading and sorting words with 'ee' spellings

e	ee	ea	y	ey

sea	feet	we	funny
key	penny	week	leaf
alley	jockey	sheep	happy
treat	feed	plenty	begin
trolley	she	sweet	lucky
easy	teach	creep	secret
heat	body	betray	steam
donkey	Greek	me	greedy

Teaching guidelines: Photocopy this page onto card and cut into reading cards. Read and sort the cards out according to the 'ee' spellings. The cards at the top of the sheet can be used as headings for each spelling. These spellings can be recorded on the following sheet.

Book 7: Spellings: 'ee'

ee

y

ea

ey

e

Teaching guidelines: List the words from the reading and sorting cards according to the spelling of the sound 'ee'.

Book 7: Reading and spelling

Two-syllable words with 'ee' spellings

Word	Read	Spelling	Spelled
s**ea**/weed	✓	_ __ /_ __ _	
a/gr**ee**		_ /_ _ __	
donk/**ey**		_ _ _ _ /__	
re/l**ea**se		_ _ /_ __ __	
chim/n**ey**		__ _ _ /_ __	
luck/**y**		_ _ __ /_	
s**e**/cret		_ _ /_ _ _ _	
dadd/**y**		_ _ __ /_	
b**e**/gin		_ _ /_ _ _	

Teaching aims: Reading and spelling words with alternative spellings of the sound 'ee'.

Teaching guidelines: Fold this sheet along the dotted line. Ask the pupil to read the words on the left and tick the words she/he has read correctly. Ask the pupil to turn over the sheet and dictate the words to the pupil. Ask the pupil to spell the words by segmenting and sounding out the sounds as she/he writes them on the lines. Ask the pupil to open the sheet and tick the words she/he has spelled correctly.

Book 7: Reading practice

Two-syllable words with 'ee' spellings words

(syllables split)

sea weed	a gree	don key
luck y	se cret	re lease
creep ing	chim ney	dadd y
dis ease	re pay	chut ney
clum sy	greed y	bean bag
tea pot	be tween	teas ing
dream ing	cherr y	Two-syllable words with 'ee' spellings (Alba Book 7)

Teaching aim: Reading practice
Teaching guidelines: Photocopy this page onto card and cut into reading cards.

Book 7: Reading practice

Two-syllable words with 'ee' spellings words

seaweed	agree	donkey
lucky	secret	release
creeping	chimney	daddy
disease	repay	chutney
clumsy	greedy	beanbag
teapot	between	teasing
dreaming	cherry	Two-syllable words with 'ee' spellings (Alba Book 7)

Teaching aim: Reading practice

Teaching guidelines: Photocopy this page onto card and cut into reading cards.

Book 7: 4-in-a-row game 'ee'

funny	delay	keep	reflex	speak
greed	being	jelly	team	green
silly	lean	stream	clean	we
free	plead	carry	happy	seem
treat	sleep	beak	dream	real
speed	sunny	we	read	beach
began	body	three	queen	holly

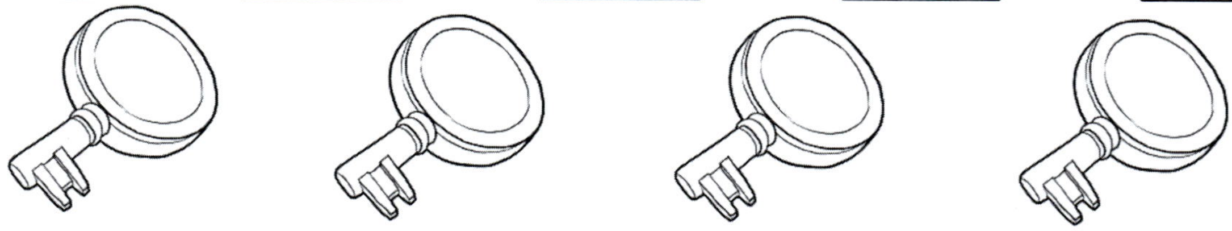

A game for two players: Play with two sets of coloured counters. Players take turns to read a word and put a counter on it. The winner is the first to get four of his or her counters in a row in any direction. The winner places a counter on a key. The game is played four times until all the keys are covered.

Book 7: Stepping stones reading game 'ee' words

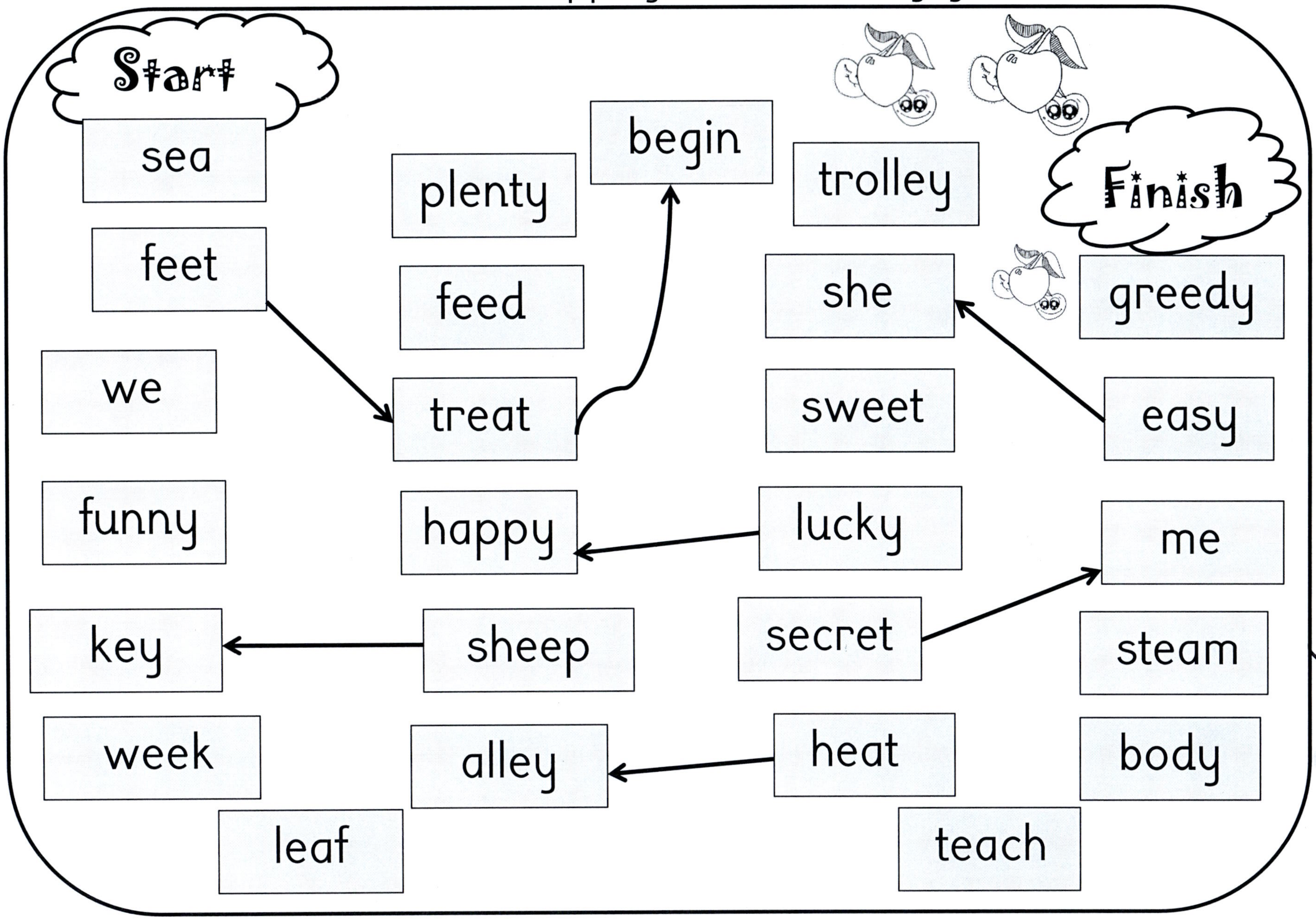

A game for 1–4 players: Play with counters and dice.
Players should read aloud the words that they land on at the end of each turn and follow the direction arrows if they land on them.

Book 7: Questions for discussion

Chapter 1

1. What is the first thing Alba sees when she opens the rusty gate? (page 2)
2. Why is the apple blossom described as being 'like whipped cream'? (page 2)
3. How does Alba feel when she sees the little stream? (page 3)

Chapter 2

1. What has happened to the old man's keys? (page 4)
2. Why does Alba chase after the old man? (page 5)

Chapter 3

1. Why is Alba frightened when she first sees the stag beetle? (page 7)
2. What do stag beetles really eat? (page 9)
3. What does Alba realise on page 10?

Chapter 4

1. Why has Alba been dreaming about apple trees? (page 11)

Teaching aims: Speaking and listening skills, comprehension and vocabulary.

Teaching guidelines: These questions can be discussed after reading the text.

Book 7: True or false?

	yes	no
Alba was next to a rusty little gate.	☐	☐
Behind the gate was a sea of plum trees.	☐	☐
Alba hopped across a stream on an old plank.	☐	☐
An old man was sipping coffee on a bench.	☐	☐
Alba picked up the man's keys.	☐	☐
A cockroach fell out of a tree next to Alba.	☐	☐
The old man bumped into the beetle.	☐	☐
Alba had been asleep and the apple trees were just a dream.	☐	☐

Teaching aim: Comprehension
Teaching guidelines: Ask the pupil to read the sentences and tick the boxes according to whether they are true or false.

Book 7: Picture the scene

Alba is leaning against a big bag of sweets.

Her bracelet is on her knee.

She is dreaming of apples.

She has a big key next to her.

Teaching aims: Following instructions, comprehension and vocabulary

Teaching guidelines: Encourage the pupil to read the text carefully and draw the details of the picture as described in the text.

Book 7: Alba's diary

I saw a sea of apple trees. A stream weaved between them. I helped an old man get his keys back. I saw a horrid beetle. In the end, the sea of trees was just a dream!

I saw a __ ___ of

__ ___ ___ __ __ ___ __. A

__ __ __ ___ __ __ ___ __ ___

__ __ __ __ ___ __ ___ __ __. I

__ __ __ __ ___ __ __ __ __ __

__ __ __ __ __ __ his __ ___ __

__ __ ___. I saw a

__ __ ___ __ __ __ ___ __ ___!

__ __ the __ __ __, the

__ ___ of __ __ ___ __ was

__ __ __ __ a __ __ ___ __!

Teaching aims: Reading and spelling activity
Teaching guidelines: Encourage the pupil to copy the text at the top and insert it into the cloze exercise below it. Pupils should write a sound on each line e.g: h e l p. This activity can also be used for dictation.

Book 7: New words

New words in Book 7

revealed – showed
weaved – moved along in a winding way to avoid obstacles
glint – a tiny flash of light
scaled – climbed up
clutched – held tightly

REMINDER – A sentence **begins** with a capital letter and **ends** with a full stop.

Alba leaned on the gate	a tree.
Alba clutched	weaved between the trees.
Alba scaled	and revealed a secret.
A little stream	a glint of metal.
Alba spotted	the apple pip as she set off.

Teaching aims: This activity includes new vocabulary introduced in Book 7. It encourages the pupil to think about the meaning of the new words and to use them to construct a complete sentence.
Teaching guidelines: Cut the sentences into strips and cut along the centre line. Ask the pupil to match the two parts of the sentence so that they make sense. The pupil may need a reminder of what the words mean.

Book 7: Postcard home

Dear Mum,

First

Then

In the end

Love from Alba xxx

Teaching aims: Comprehension and free writing

Teaching guidelines: Encourage the pupil to write about what happened in Book 7. The sentence starters provide useful cues for breaking the story into sections. Useful words are provided at the bottom of the page. The teacher can decide whether or not to offer these.

Useful words: secret stream key beetle dream

Book 7: Punctuation

Capital letters and full stops

REMINDER – A sentence **begins** with a capital letter and **ends** with a full stop.

alba spotted a rusty gate she leaned against it she revealed a sea of apple trees alba leapfrogged across a little stream

an old man was reading on a bench and drinking tea when he got up to leave he dropped his key alba grabbed it

a massive stag beetle dropped from the tree the old man brushed it with his sleeve it fell in the mud alba was back in the street she had been asleep the apple trees had just been a dream

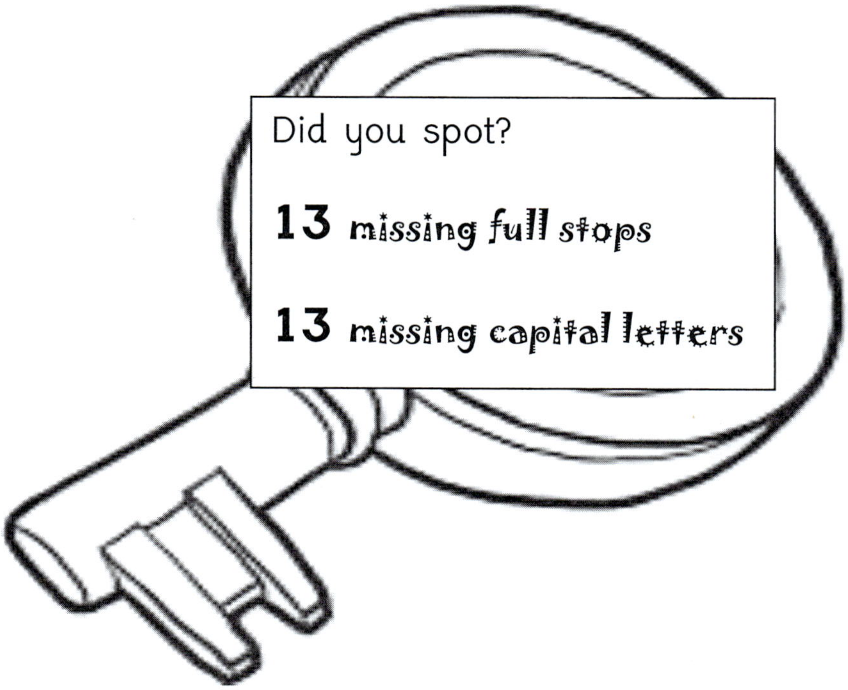

Did you spot?

13 *missing full stops*

13 *missing capital letters*

Book 8: The Long Road Home

Phonic focus: 'oe' **Spellings:** o, ow, oa, o–e

Contents

Book 8: Word-building 'oe' words

c	oa	t
c	*oa*	*t*

Teaching aims:

- learn the spelling alternatives <oa>, <ow> and <o> for the sound 'oe'
- be able to segment and blend words with these three different spellings

Teaching guidelines:

Use a white board on which three lines have been drawn. Print cards from the appendix for the spellings <oa>, <ow> and <o>. Add these to the cards with the letters of the alphabet from previous levels.
Teachers can choose whether to start work with one spelling of the sound or whether to begin with multiple spellings.

Teach word-building with the spellings <oa>, <ow> and <o>:

Select a word from the lists below. Use only the letters needed to build that word and jumble them up. Ask the pupil to build that word by listening to the sounds in the words and segmenting all the sounds in the words, one at a time. The pupil then brings down each card once he/she has segmented the sound in the word. Ask the pupil to read the word he/she has built. Ask the pupil to write the word under the lines, saying the sounds as he/she writes each sound. Draw more lines for longer words.

Word lists for word-building, reading and spelling:

oa	
coat	foal
road	soap
roast	groan
float	boast

ow	
blow	snow
crow	show
mow	flow
grow	throw

o	
no	gold
so	told
sold	hold
cold	bold

Book 8: Word–building ‘o–e’ words

n [ ] t [ ] ___ ___ ___ ___

h [ ] p [ ] ___ ___ ___ ___

b [ ] n [ ] ___ ___ ___ ___

m [ ] l [ ] ___ ___ ___ ___

d r [ ] v [ ] ___ ___ ___ ___ ___

s l [ ] p [ ] ___ ___ ___ ___ ___

o	e	o	e	o	e	o	e	o	e	o	e

Teaching aims:

- learn the spelling <o–e>for the sound ‘oe’
- be able to segment and blend words with this spelling

Teaching guidelines:

Cut out the ‘oe’ cards. Ask the pupil to cut along the central line in the spelling cards and insert the split spelling of the ‘oe’ in the words above. Ask the pupil to say the sounds as they blend them into a word and then write the word on the lines, saying the sounds as they do.

Book 8: Timed reading 'o–e' words

Beat your own record!

cod	code	dot	dote	hop	hope	not	note
slop	slope	rob	robe	mop	mope	rod	rode
Dom	dome	rot	rote	doll	dole	glob	globe
tot	tote	lob	lobe	con	cone		

spoke	joke	top	plot	bone	not	drop	clone
blob	lone	rode	tot	drove	cot	lob	clove
smoke	flop	hope	those	from	dose	vote	
cop	stone	rot	rose	plot	tone	clot	home

Teaching guidelines: Ask the pupil to read the text as fast as possible to try to beat his/her own time. Yo[u] will need a timer for this activity.

Book 8: Reading and spelling 'oe' words with <o> and <o–e> spellings

go	✓
so	
roll	
cold	

__ __	
__ __	
__ __ ____	
__ __ __ __	

bone	
code	
vote	
spoke	

__ __ __ __	
__ __ __ __	
__ __ __ __	
__ __ __ __ __	

Teaching aims: Reading and spelling 'oe' words with the spellings <o> and <o–e>.

Teaching guidelines: Fold this sheet along the dotted line. Ask the pupil to read the words on the left and tick the words she/he has read correctly. Ask the pupil to turn over the sheet and dictate the words to the pupil. Ask the pupil to spell the words by segmenting and sounding out the sounds as she/he writes them on the lines. Ask the pupil to open the sheet and tick the words she/he has spelled correctly.

Book 8: Reading and spelling 'oe' words with <oa> and <ow> spellings

Word	Tick
boat	✓
moan	
road	
coast	

Spelling	Tick
__ ____ __	
__ ____ __	
__ ____ __	
__ ____ __ __	

Word	Tick
bowl	
glow	
show	
crow	

Spelling	Tick
__ ____ __	
__ __ ____	
____ ____	
__ __ ____	

Teaching aims: Reading and spelling 'oe' words with the spellings <oa> and <ow>.

Teaching guidelines: Fold this sheet along the dotted line. Ask the pupil to read the words on the left and tick the words she/he has read correctly. Ask the pupil to turn over the sheet and dictate the words to the pupil. Ask the pupil to spell the words by segmenting and sounding out the sounds as she/he writes them on the lines. Ask the pupil to open the sheet and tick the words she/he has spelled correctly.

Book 8: Reading and sorting words with 'oe' spellings

oa	ow	o	o–e

noble	road	slow	goal
home	gold	boat	row
foam	folded	stone	roast
glowing	moaned	sold	bone
soap	crow	loaf	Rome
dozing	floated	joke	bowl
coal	slope	arrow	loan
toast	stove	old	show

Teaching guidelines: Photocopy this page onto card and cut into reading cards. Read and sort the cards out according to the 'oe' spellings. The cards at the top of the sheet can be used as headings for each spelling. These spellings can be recorded on the following sheet.

Book 8: Spellings: 'oe'

oa

o–e

ow

o

Teaching guidelines: List the words from the reading and sorting cards according to the spelling of the sound 'oe'.

Book 8: Reading and spelling

Two-syllable words with 'oe' spellings

n**o**s**e**/bleed	✓
gr**ow**/ing	
r**oa**d/block	
yell/**ow**	
r**o**/bot	
trom/b**o**n**e**	
a/ppr**oa**ch	
br**o**/ken	
sn**ow**/man	

Teaching aims: Reading and spelling words with alternative spellings of the sound 'oe'.

Teaching guidelines: Fold this sheet along the dotted line. Ask the pupil to read the words on the left and tick the words she/he has read correctly. Ask the pupil to turn over the sheet and dictate the words to the pupil. Ask the pupil to spell the words by segmenting and sounding out the sounds as she/he writes them on the lines. Ask the pupil to open the sheet and tick the words she/he has spelled correctly.

Book 8: Reading practice

Two-syllable words with 'oe' spellings words

(syllables split)

a **lone**	a ppr**oa**ch	borr **ow**
trom **bone**	sn**ow** flake	br**o** ken
r**oa**d block	n**o** mad	may **pole**
gr**ow** bag	cheek **bone**	n**ose** band
yell **ow**	r**o** bot	fish b**ow**l
sn**ow** ing	peep **hole**	re **mote**
con tr**o**l	p**o**st box	Two-syllable words with 'oe' spellings (Alba Book 8)

Teaching aim: Reading practice

Teaching guidelines: Photocopy this page onto card and cut into reading cards.

Two-syllable words with 'oe' spellings words

alone	approach	borrow
trombone	snowflake	broken
roadblock	nomad	maypole
growbag	cheekbone	noseband
yellow	robot	fishbowl
snowing	peephole	remote
control	postbox	Two-syllable words with 'oe' spellings (Alba Book 8)

Teaching aim: Reading practice

Teaching guidelines: Photocopy this page onto card and cut into reading cards.

Book 8: 4-in-a-row game 'oe'

show	hold	joke	coach	flow
tone	moan	code	glow	road
sold	blow	goat	go	hope
coast	gold	stone	elbow	roll
bolt	bowl	groan	Rome	home
stove	soak	fold	own	loaf
throw	no	stole	soap	row

A game for two players: Play with two sets of coloured counters. Players take turns to read a word and put a counter on it. The winner is the first to get four of his or her counters in a row in any direction. The winner places a counter on a dog. The game is played four times until all the dogs are covered.

Book 8: Stepping stones reading game ‘oe’ words

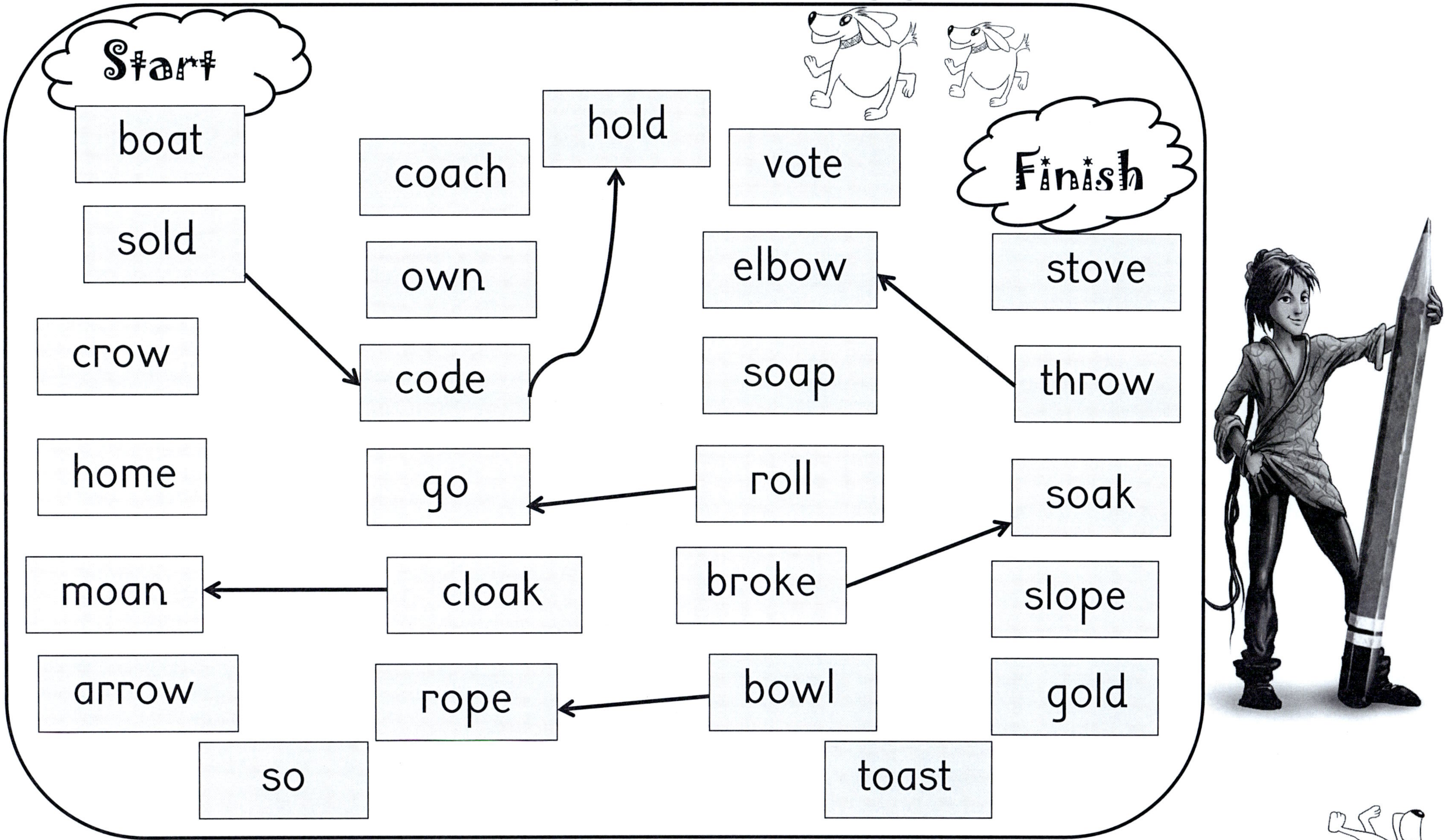

A game for 1–4 players: Play with counters and dice.
Players should read aloud the words that they land on at the end of each turn and follow the direction arrows if they land on them.

Book 8: Questions for discussion

Chapter 1

1. Why is Alba feeling a little sad at the start of the story? (pages 1 and 2)
2. What does she use to help her rest on the stony ground? (page 3)

Chapter 2

1. Why does Alba feel filled with hope when she finds the mobile phone? (page 4)
2. Why do you think the broken phone makes her feel even more lonely? (page 5)

Chapter 3

1. Why does Alba decide to climb up onto the dog's back? (page 8)
2. Why does Alba feel cold when she is on his back? (page 9)

Chapter 4

1. Why do you think Alba feels the dog has given her hope? (page 11)

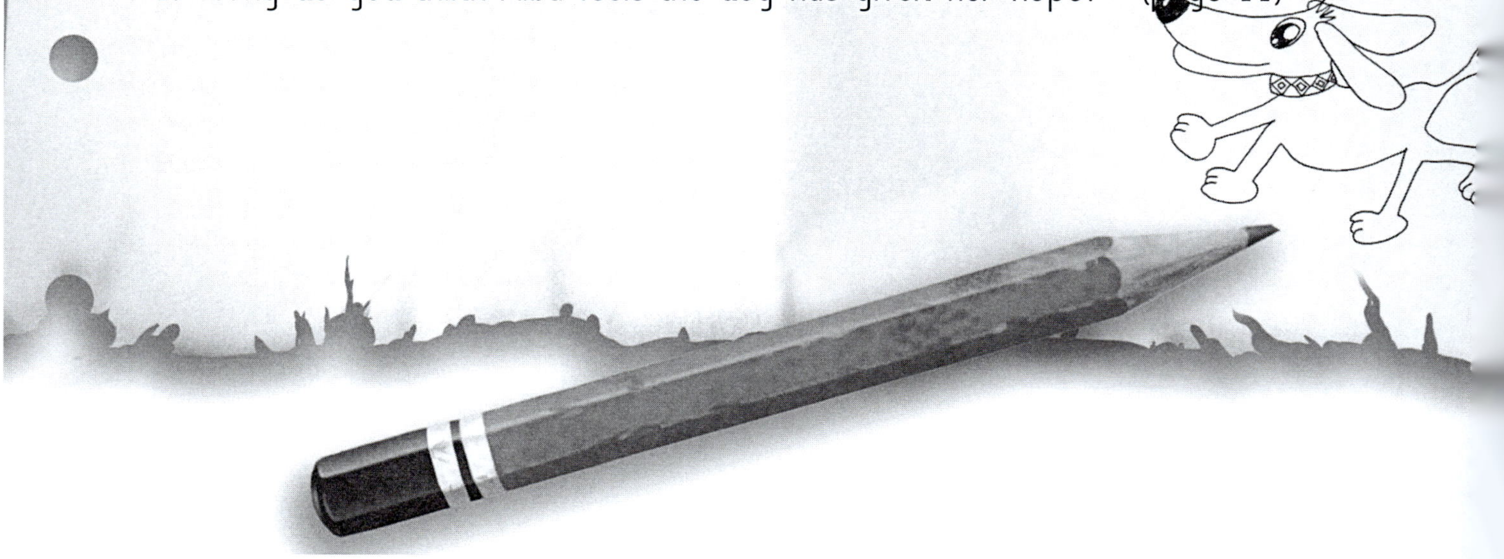

Teaching aims: Speaking and listening skills, comprehension and vocabulary.

Teaching guidelines: These questions can be discussed after reading the text

Book 8: True or false?

	yes	no
Alba was at the top of a slope of grass.		
Lots of apple trees had grown on the slope.		
A bumble bee woke Alba up.		
Alba used the mobile phone to ring her dad.		
The dog bit Alba when she approached him.		
Alba rode down the hill on the dog's back.		
It was hot and sunny as she rode along.		
Alba gave the dog a bone when she jumped off his back.		

Teaching aim: Comprehension
Teaching guidelines: Ask the pupil to read the sentences and tick the boxes according to whether they are true or false.

Book 8: Picture the scene

Alba is sitting on top of the dog.

She is holding onto his thick collar.

Leaves are blowing in the wind.

The dog is dreaming about a big, tasty bone.

Teaching aims: Following instructions, comprehension and vocabulary

Teaching guidelines: Encourage the pupil to read the text carefully and draw the details of the picture as described in the text.

Book 8: Alba's diary

I stopped to rest at the top of a slope. A big dog approached me! The dog let me get up on his back. I rode down the hill on his back. It was so cold!

I _ _ _ _ _ to _ _ _ _

_ _ the _ _ _ of a

_ _ _ _ _. A _ _ _ _ _ _

_ _ _ _ _ _ _ _! The

_ _ _ _ _ _ _ _ _ _ _

_ _ _ _ _ _ _ _ _ _.

I _ _ _ _ down the

_ _ _ _ _ _ _ _ _ _ _.

_ _ was _ _ _ _ _ _!

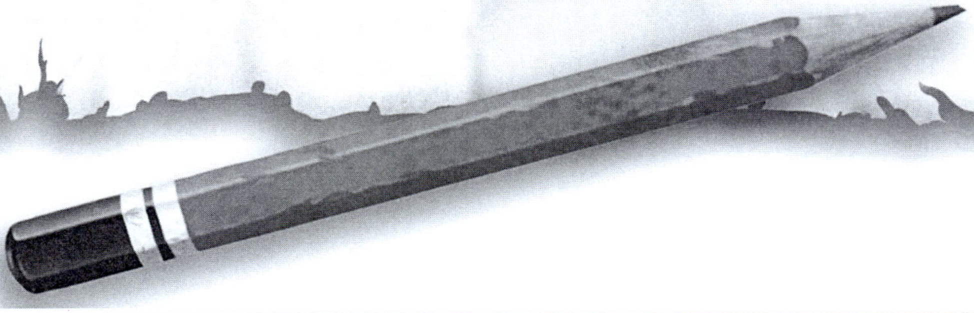

Teaching aims: Reading and spelling activity
Teaching guidelines: Encourage the pupil to copy the text at the top and insert it into the cloze exercise below it. Pupils should write a sound on each line e.g: h e l p. This activity can also be used for dictation.

Book 8: New words

New words in Book 8

drone – a dull buzzing sound
sorrow – sadness or regret
approached – came near to
glow – feeling of warmth or heat
boldly – bravely and without fear

REMINDER – A sentence **begins** with a capital letter and **ends** with a full stop.

A low drone	made Alba's face glow.

The cold wind	approached Alba.

Alba set off boldly	woke Alba up.

Alba was filled with sorrow	along the road.

An old dog	that the phone was broken.

Teaching aims: This activity includes new vocabulary introduced in Book 8. It encourages the pupil to think about the meaning of the new words and to use them to construct a complete sentence.
Teaching guidelines: Cut the sentences into strips and cut along the centre line. Ask the pupil to match the two parts of the sentence so that they make sense. The pupil may need a reminder of what the words mean.

Book 8: Postcard home

Dear Mum,

First

Then

In the end

Love from Alba xxx

Teaching aims: Comprehension and free writing

Teaching guidelines: Encourage the pupil to write about what happened in Book 8. The sentence starters provide useful cues for breaking the story into sections. Useful words are provided at the bottom of the page. The teacher can decide whether or not to offer these.

Useful words: lonely mobile phone approached stroke

Book 8: Punctuation

Capital letters and full stops

REMINDER – A sentence **begins** with a capital letter and **ends** with a full stop.

alba stopped to rest at the top of a slope she was still a long way from home she felt lonely and homesick

a mobile phone woke alba up she was so sad when she saw that it was broken an old dog approached alba

alba rode the dog down the slope the dog ran as fast as the wind when they reached the bottom of the slope alba rolled off the dog she stroked him as she left

Book 9: Supper

Phonic focus: phoneme 'er' **Spellings:** er, ir, ur

Contents

Book 9: Word-building 'er' words

b	ir	d
b	*ir*	*d*

Teaching aims:

- learn the spelling alternatives <er>, <ir> and <ur> for the sound 'er'
- be able to segment and blend words with these three different spellings

Teaching guidelines:

Use a white board on which three lines have been drawn. Print cards from the appendix for the spellings <er>, <ir> and <ur>. Add these to the cards with the letters of the alphabet from previous levels. Additional lines should be drawn for longer words.

Teachers can choose whether to start work with one spelling of the sound or whether to begin with multiple spellings.

Teach word-building with the spellings <er>, <ir> and <ur>:

Select a word from the lists below. Use only the letters needed to build that word and jumble them up. Ask the pupil to build that word by listening to the sounds in the words and segmenting all the sounds in the words, one at a time. The pupil then brings down each card once he/she has segmented the sound in the word. Ask the pupil to read the word he/she has built. Ask the pupil to write the word under the lines, saying the sounds as he/she writes each sound. Draw more lines for longer words.

Word lists for word-building, reading and spelling:

er	
herb	verb
perk	jerk
term	herd
kerb	stern

ir	
dirt	girl
stir	bird
third	shirt
skirt	birth

ur	
turn	burn
curl	hurt
turf	surf
lurk	church

Book 9: Reading and spelling 'er' words with <er>, <ir> and <ur> spellings

verb	✓
germ	
stern	

bird	
girl	
first	

hurt	
lurk	
church	

Teaching aims: Reading and spelling 'er' words with the spellings <er>, <ir> and <ur>.

Teaching guidelines: Fold this sheet along the dotted line. Ask the pupil to read the words on the left and tick the words she/he has read correctly. Ask the pupil to turn over the sheet and dictate the words to the pupil. Ask the pupil to spell the words by segmenting and sounding out the sounds as she/he writes them on the lines. Ask the pupil to open the sheet and tick the words she/he has spelled correctly.

Book 9: Reading and sorting words with 'er' spellings

er	ir	ur

verb	curve	squirt	swerve
birth	berth	urn	bird
fern	turn	dirt	germ
turf	shirt	her	surf
first	herb	purse	firm
herd	lurk	girl	jerk
nurse	third	kerb	hurt
skirt	nerve	fur	stir

Teaching guidelines: Photocopy this page onto card and cut into reading cards. Read and sort the cards out according to the 'er' spellings. The cards at the top of the sheet can be used as headings for each spelling. These spellings can be recorded on the following sheet.

Book 9: Spellings: 'er'

er	ir	ur

Teaching guidelines: List the words from the reading and sorting cards according to the spelling of the sound 'er'.

Book 9: Reading and spelling

Two-syllable words with 'er' spellings

black/b**ir**d	✓	_ _ _ __/_ __ _	
f**ur**/nish		_ __/_ _ __	
dust/**er**		_ _ _ _/__	
dis/t**ur**b		_ _ _/_ __ _	
tum/bl**er**		_ __/_ _ __	
th**ir**/teen		__ __/_ __ _	
splin/t**er**		_ _ _ _ _/_ __	
b**ir**th/day		_ __ __/_ __	
Th**urs**/day		__ __ _/_ __	

Teaching aims: Reading and spelling words with alternative spellings of the sound 'er'.

Teaching guidelines: Fold this sheet along the dotted line. Ask the pupil to read the words on the left and tick the words she/he has read correctly. Ask the pupil to turn over the sheet and dictate the words to the pupil. Ask the pupil to spell the words by segmenting and sounding out the sounds as she/he writes them on the lines. Ask the pupil to open the sheet and tick the words she/he has spelled correctly.

Book 9: Reading practice

Two-syllable words with ‘er’ spellings

(syllables split)

ab surd	birth day	bur ger
cir cus	des ert	fur ther
ur ban	cur ly	firm ly
her mit	burn ing	stur dy
gur gle	fur nish	dir ty
runn er	mur der	per fect
thir sty	a lert	Two-syllable words with ‘er’ spellings (Alba Book 9)

Teaching aim: Reading practice

Teaching guidelines: Photocopy this page onto card and cut into reading cards.

Book 9: Reading practice

Two-syllable words with 'er' spellings

absurd	birthday	burger
circus	desert	further
urban	curly	firmly
hermit	burning	sturdy
gurgle	furnish	dirty
runner	murder	perfect
thirsty	alert	Two-syllable words with 'er' spellings (Alba Book 9)

Teaching aim: Reading practice

Teaching guidelines: Photocopy this page onto card and cut into reading cards.

Book 9: 4-in-a-row game 'er'

silver	hurdle	perm	skirt	firm
burn	term	curb	stir	herb
girl	turnip	older	nurse	shirt
her	curve	bird	serve	churn
lurk	swirl	kerb	squirt	twirl
dirt	finger	first	anger	burst
quirky	blur	fur	fir	curl

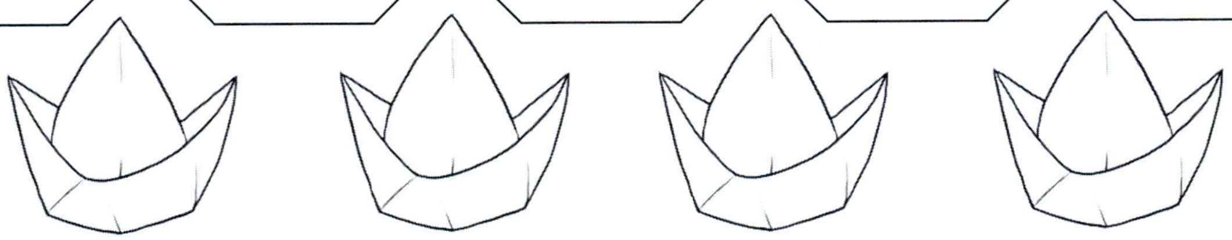

A game for two players: Play with two sets of coloured counters. Players take turns to read a word and put a counter on it. The winner is the first to get four of his or her counters in a row in any direction. The winner places a counter on a boat. The game is played four times until all the boats are covered.

Book 9: Stepping stones reading game 'er' words

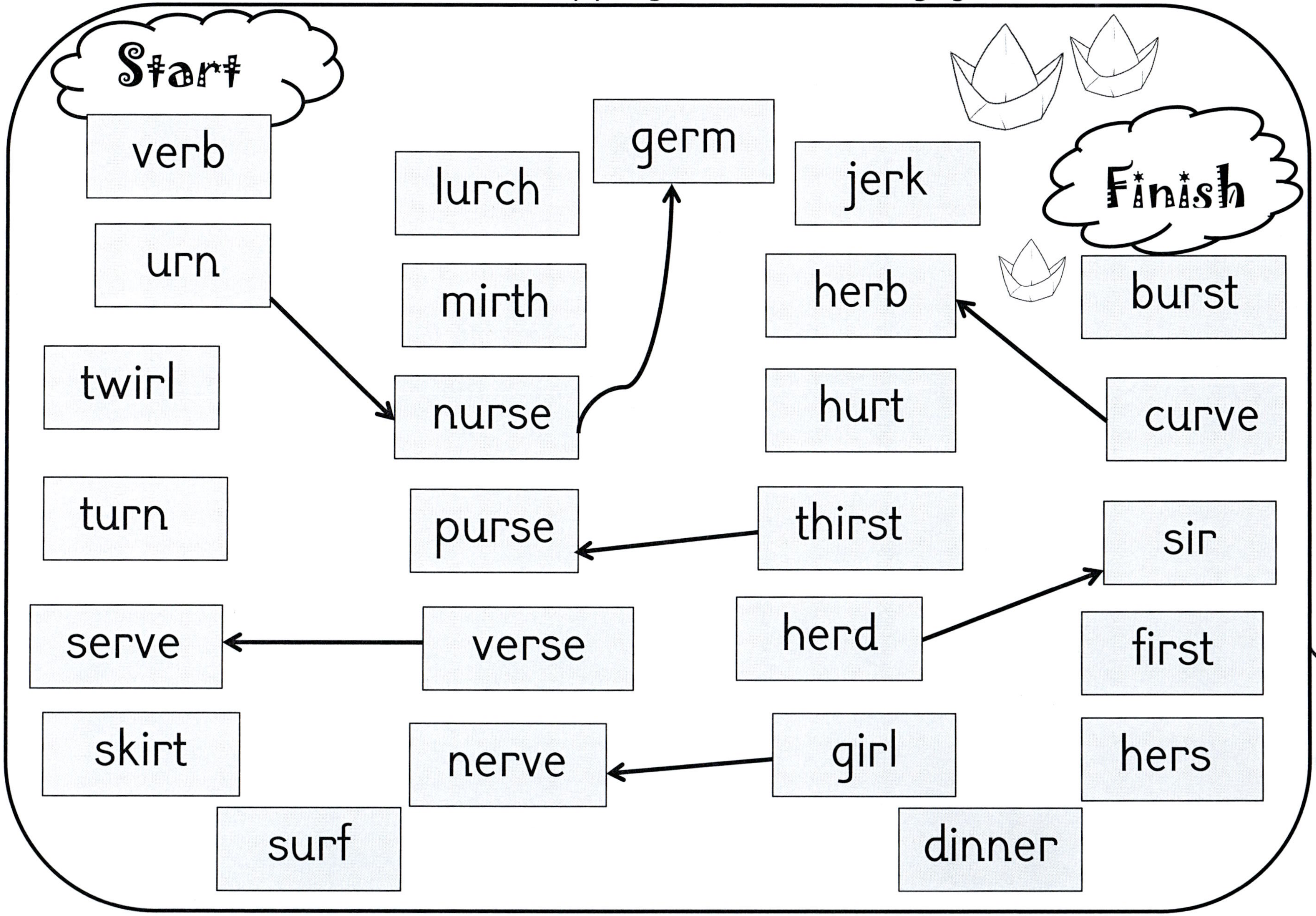

A game for 1–4 players: Play with counters and dice.
Players should read aloud the words that they land on at the end of each turn and follow the direction arrows if they land on them.

Book 9: Questions for discussion

Chapter 1

1. How is Alba feeling at the beginning of the story? (page 1)
2. Where does she stop to rest? Why is it a good choice? (page 2)
3. How does Alba feel when she sees the money in the letter? (page 3)

Chapter 2

1. Why is the water described as 'gurgling' in the gutter? (page 4)
2. Why does Alba want to avoid the cat and her kittens? (page 6)

Chapter 3

1. Why is Alba excited when she first sees the two sisters? (page 9)
2. How does Alba get a drink? (page 10)

Chapter 4

1. Why is Alba keen to get to the river? (page 12)

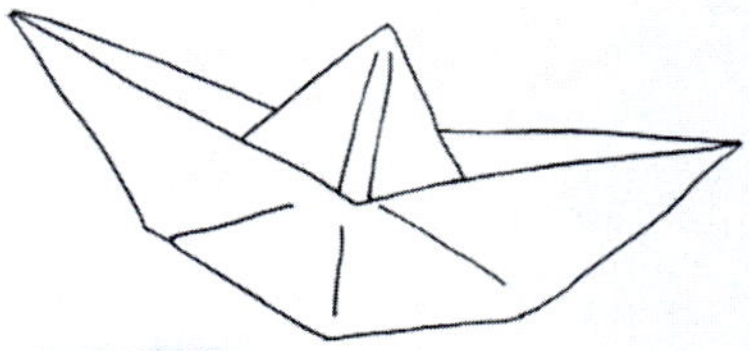

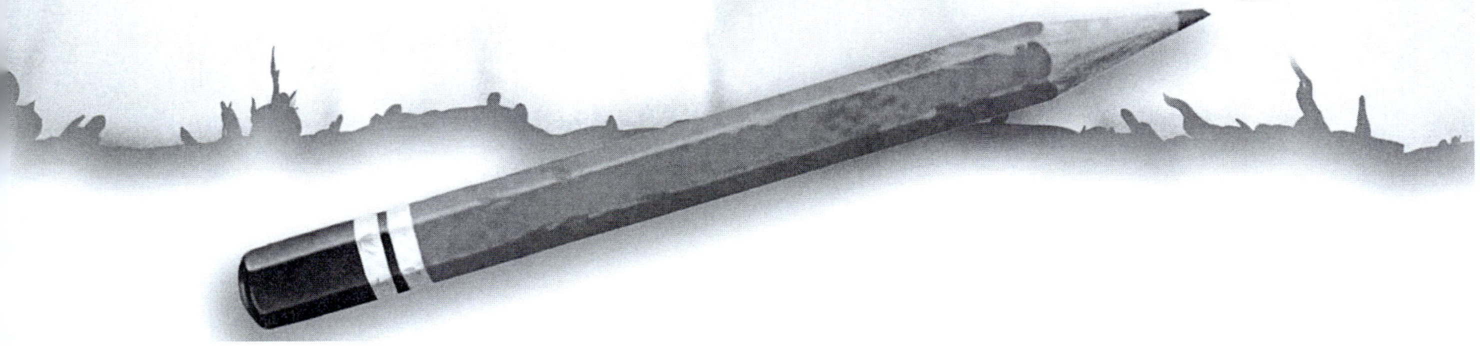

Teaching aims: Speaking and listening skills, comprehension and vocabulary.

Teaching guidelines: These questions can be discussed after reading the text.

Book 9: True or false?

	yes	no
Alba was hungry and thirsty.		
Alba stopped to shelter from the rain.		
A letter had some cash in it.		
Alba needed the cash to get a raincoat.		
Alba folded the letter into a paper boat.		
She sailed past a little puppy.		
Alba was hurled into the dirty water.		
Alba rolled an apple at a tumbler of water.		

Teaching aim: Comprehension
Teaching guidelines: Ask the pupil to read the sentences and tick the boxes according to whether they are true or false.

Book 9: Picture the scene

Alba is standing in a paper boat.

There is water under the boat.

Alba is holding a stick.

She has a bracelet on.

There is a flower on top of the water.

Teaching aims: Following instructions, comprehension and vocabulary

Teaching guidelines: Encourage the pupil to read the text carefully and draw the details of the picture as described in the text.

Book 9: Alba's diary

I found some cash in a letter under a fern. I made the letter into a paper boat. I sailed it along the gutter. I fell in the dirty water. I ate a bun with ham and butter.

I found some _ _ __ _ _

a _ _ __ __ _ _ _ __ a

_ __ _. I _ _ _ _ the

_ _ __ __ into a _ _ _

_ __ _. I _ __ _ __ _ _

_ _ _ __ the _ _ __ __. I

_ _ __ _ _ the _ __ _ _

water. I _ _ _ a _ _ _

_ _ __ _ _ _ _ _ _

_ _ __ __.

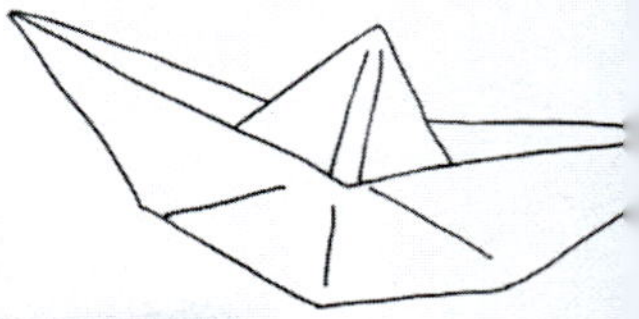

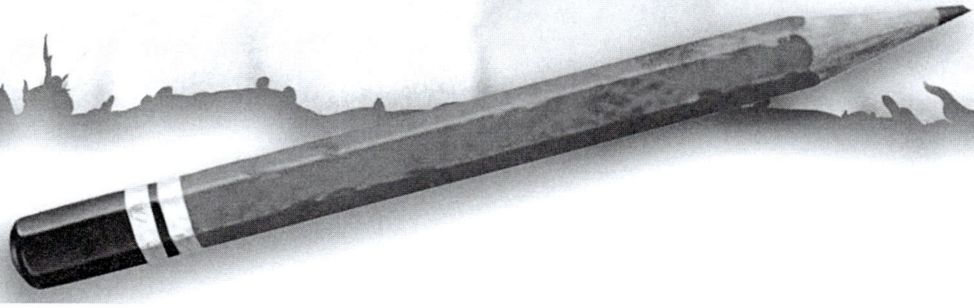

Teaching aims: Reading and spelling activity
Teaching guidelines: Encourage the pupil to copy the text at the top and insert it into the cloze exercise below it. Pupils should write a sound on each line e.g: h e l p. This activity can also be used for dictation.

Book 9: New words

New words in Book 9

gurgled – flowed noisily
swerved – changed direction suddenly
sturdy – strong
hamper – a large basket
hurled – threw with great force

REMINDER – A sentence **begins** with a capital letter and **ends** with a full stop.

The water gurgled	a big picnic hamper.

Alba swerved	in the gutter.

She grabbed hold of	into the freezing water.

The sisters had	the boat away from the cats.

Alba was hurled	a sturdy stick.

Teaching aims: This activity includes new vocabulary introduced in Book 9. It encourages the pupil to think about the meaning of the new words and to use them to construct a complete sentence.
Teaching guidelines: Cut the sentences into strips and cut along the centre line. Ask the pupil to match the two parts of the sentence so that they make sense. The pupil may need a reminder of what the words mean.

Book 9: Postcard home

Dear Mum,

First

Then

In the end

Love from Alba xxx

Teaching aims: Comprehension and free writing

Teaching guidelines: Encourage the pupil to write about what happened in Book 9. The sentence starters provide useful cues for breaking the story into sections. Useful words are provided at the bottom of the page. The teacher can decide whether or not to offer these.

useful words: thirsty shelter letter paper hurled hamper

Book 9: Punctuation

Capital letters and full stops

REMINDER – A sentence **begins** with a capital letter and **ends** with a full stop.

the sun is up and it is hot alba stops to shelter under a fern she spots a letter

the letter has cash in it alba needs the cash to get her supper she makes the letter into a paper boat

alba is hurled into the water a sturdy stick saves her and she gets to the kerb she has supper from a picnic hamper

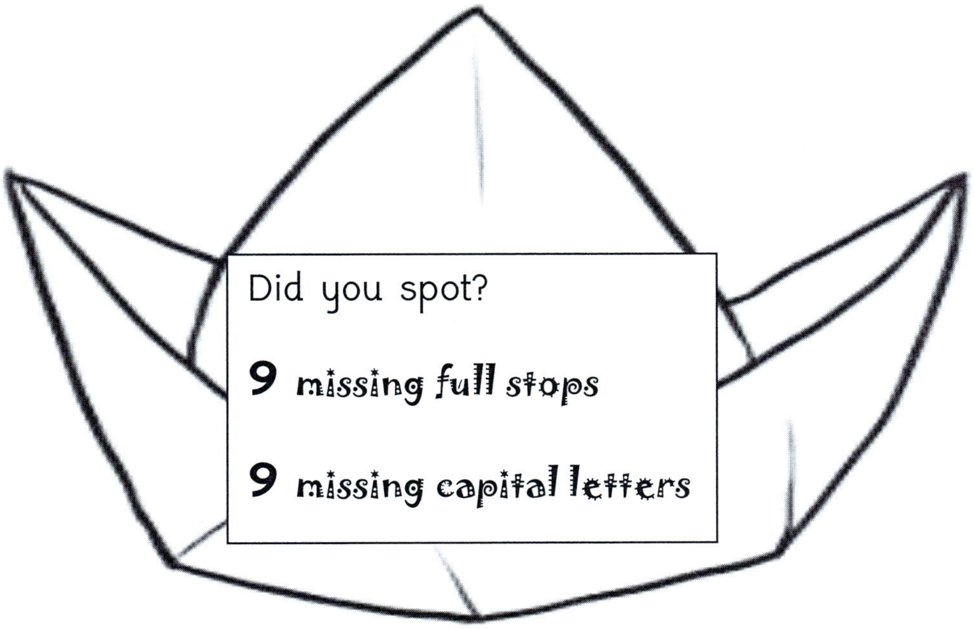

Book 10: Howling Wind

Phonic focus: phoneme 'ow' **Spellings:** ow, ou

Contents

Book 10: Word-building 'ow' words

t	ow	n
t	*ow*	*n*

Teaching aims:

- learn the spelling alternatives <ou> and <ow> for the sound 'ow'
- be able to segment and blend words with these three different spellings

Teacher guidelines:

Use a white board on which three lines have been drawn. Print cards from the appendix for the spellings <ou> and <ow>. Add these to the cards with the letters of the alphabet from previous levels.

Teachers can choose whether to start work with one spelling of the sound or whether to begin with multiple spellings.

Additional lines should be drawn for words with longer spellings (i.e. crowd).

Teach word-building with the spellings <ou> and <ow>:

Select a word from the lists below. Use only the letters needed to build that word and jumble them up. Ask the pupil to build that word by listening to the sounds in the words and segmenting all the sounds in the words, one at a time. The pupil then brings down each card once he/she has segmented the sound in the word. Ask the pupil to read the word he/she has built. Ask the pupil to write the word under the lines, saying the sounds as he/she writes each sound.

Word lists for word-building, reading and spelling:

ou	
loud	pout
cloud	found
scout	count
crouch	ground

ow	
cow	now
down	town
growl	crowd
scowl	clown

Book 10: Reading and spelling 'ow' words with <ou> and <ow> spellings

loud	✓	___ ___ ___	
shout		___ ___ ___	
mouth		___ ___ ___	
ground		___ ___ ___ ___ ___	

town		___ ___ ___	
brow		___ ___ ___	
growl		___ ___ ___ ___	
crown		___ ___ ___ ___	

Teaching aims: Reading and spelling 'ow' words with the spellings <ou> and <ow>.

Teaching guidelines: Fold this sheet along the dotted line. Ask the pupil to read the words on the left and tick the words she/he has read correctly. Ask the pupil to turn over the sheet and dictate the words to the pupil. Ask the pupil to spell the words by segmenting and sounding out the sounds as she/he writes them on the lines. Ask the pupil to open the sheet and tick the words she/he has spelled correctly.

Book 10: Reading and sorting words with 'ow' spellings

ow	ou

shout	snout	cow	down
growl	pout	fowl	scout
round	gown	trout	pouch
crowd	found	scowl	crown
ground	pound	mouse	now
how	row	mouth	mound
count	cloud	brow	town
crouch	clown	house	brown

Teaching guidelines: Photocopy this page onto card and cut into reading cards. Read and sort the cards out according to the 'ow' spellings. The cards at the top of the sheet can be used as headings for each spelling. These spellings can be recorded on the following sheet.

Book 10: Spellings: 'ow'

ou

ow

Teaching guidelines: List the words from the reading and sorting cards according to the spelling of the sound 'ow'.

Book 10: Reading and spelling

Two-syllable words with ‘ow’ spellings

Word	Read	Spell	Spelled
v**ou**/cher	✓	_ ___/___ ___	
cl**ou**d/less		_ _ ___ _/_ _ ___	
p**ow**/der		___/_ ___	
r**ou**n/ders		___ _/_ ___ _	
d**ow**n/hill		_ ___ _/_ _ ___	
dis/c**ou**nt		_ _ _/_ ___ _ _	
c**ow**/shed		_ ___/___ _ _	
a/r**ou**nd		_/_ ___ _ _	
l**ou**d/ly		_ ___ _/_ _	

Teaching aims: Reading and spelling words with alternative spellings of the sound ‘ow’.

Teaching guidelines: Fold this sheet along the dotted line. Ask the pupil to read the words on the left and tick the words she/he has read correctly. Ask the pupil to turn over the sheet and dictate the words to the pupil. Ask the pupil to spell the words by segmenting and sounding out the sounds as she/he writes them on the lines. Ask the pupil to open the sheet and tick the words she/he has spelled correctly.

Book 10: Reading practice

Two-syllable words with ‘ow’ spellings

(syllables split)

out ing	m**ou**nt ed	t**ow** er
tr**ou** sers	a ll**ow**ed	cl**ou**d y
c**ow** shed	l**ou**d est	**out** burst
f**ou**nd ed	d**ow**n hill	c**ou**nt d**ow**n
out fit	p**ow** der	th**ou** sand
pr**ow** ling	r**ou**nd ers	v**ou** cher
pr**ou**d ly	sh**ow** er	Two-syllable words with ‘ow’ spellings (Alba Book 10)

Teaching aim: Reading practice

Teaching guidelines: Photocopy this page onto card and cut into reading cards.

Book 10: Reading practice

Two-syllable words with 'ow' spellings

outing	mounted	tower
trousers	allowed	cloudy
cowshed	loudest	outburst
founded	downhill	countdown
outfit	powder	thousand
prowling	rounders	voucher
proudly	shower	Two-syllable words with 'ow' spellings (Alba Book 10)

Teaching aim: Reading practice

Teaching guidelines: Photocopy this page onto card and cut into reading cards.

Book 10: 4-in-a-row game 'ow'

brow	cloud	frown	couch	foul
crowd	cow	down	proud	vow
town	shout	vouch	clown	south
snout	scowl	spout	trout	crouch
round	crown	scout	pound	drown
prowl	noun	out	frown	mouse
found	growl	house	how	owl

A game for two players: Play with two sets of coloured counters. Players take turns to read a word and put a counter on it. The winner is the first to get four of his or her counters in a row in any direction. The winner places a counter on a flower. The game is played four times until all the flowers are covered.

Book 10: Stepping stones reading game 'ow' words

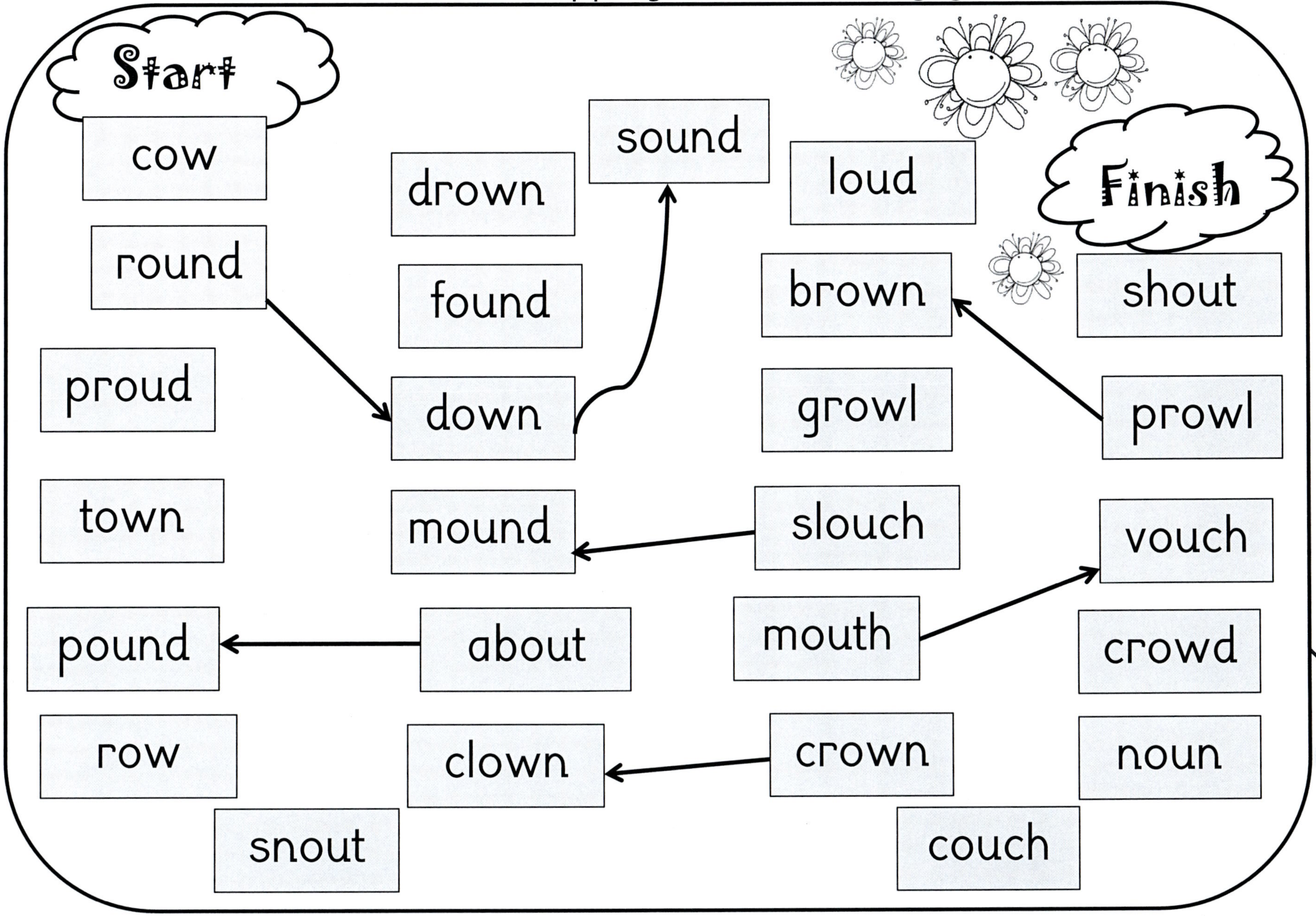

A game for 1–4 players: Play with counters and dice.
Players should read aloud the words that they land on at the end of each turn and follow the direction arrows if they land on them.

Book 10: Questions for discussion

Chapter 1

1. Why is the wind difficult when you are as small as Alba? (page 1)
2. How will the scrap of cloth help her? (page 3)

Chapter 2

1. Why does the toy car seem so big to Alba? (page 4)
2. How does the scrap of cloth help Alba when she is on the toy car? (page 6)

Chapter 3

1. What happens to the pip? (page 8)
2. Why do you think Alba's chest is pounding? What was she afraid of? (page 9)

Chapter 4

1. Why does Alba stop 'clowning around' when she sees the river? (page 11)
2. Why does Alba need a plan at the end of the story? (page 12)

Teaching aims: Speaking and listening skills, comprehension and vocabulary.

Teaching guidelines: These questions can be discussed after reading the text.

Book 10: True or false?

	yes	no
Alba hated being in the cold wind.		
Alba found a napkin on the ground.		
Alba found herself next to a toy boat.		
A brown cat ran out of the shrubs.		
Alba held the scrap of cloth up like a sail.		
Alba's bag landed in a muddy puddle.		
Alba had fun making a crown of flowers.		
When Alba saw the river, she felt a little afraid.		

Teaching aim: Comprehension
Teaching guidelines: Ask the pupil to read the sentences and tick the boxes according to whether they are true or false.

Book 10: Picture the scene

Alba has made a crown of flowers.

It has six flowers with round petals.

It has three flowers with long, thin petals.

There are seven leaves at the bottom of the crown.

A little mouse is sitting next to it.

Teaching aims: Following instructions, comprehension and vocabulary

Teaching guidelines: Encourage the pupil to read the text carefully and draw the details of the picture as described in the text.

Book 10: Alba's diary

A cold wind was sweeping around. I found a toy car and the wind swept me along the ground in it. I lost the pip in the wind but found it again.

A _ _ _ _ _ _ _ _ was

_ _ _ _ _ _ _ _ _ _ _.

I _ _ _ _ a toy car

_ _ _ the _ _ _ _

_ _ _ _ _ _ _ _ _ _ _

the _ _ _ _ _ _ _ _ _.

I _ _ _ _ the _ _ _ _ _

the _ _ _ _ _ _ _

_ _ _ _ _ _ _ _ _ _.

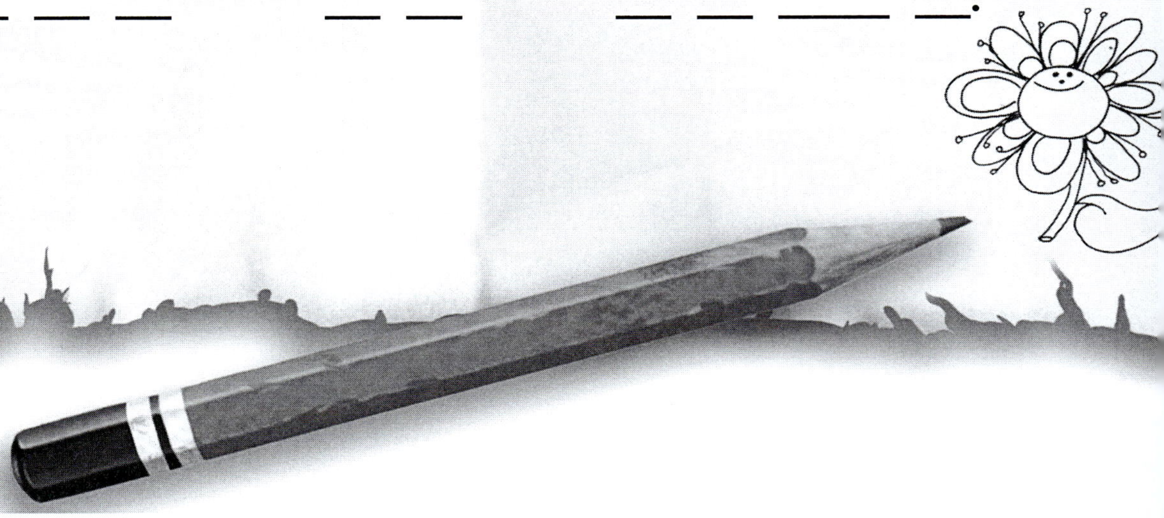

Teaching aims: Reading and spelling activity
Teaching guidelines: Encourage the pupil to copy the text at the top and insert it into the cloze exercise below it. Pupils should write a sound on each line e.g: h e l p. This activity can also be used for dictation.

Book 10: New words

New words in Book 10

crouched – stooped or bent low
prowling – searching for something to steal or someone to attack
pounding – beating or throbbing violently
gushing – flowing with force
shuddered – trembled with fear or cold

REMINDER– A sentence **begins** with a capital letter and **ends** with a full stop.

The gushing river	was pounding.
Alba shuddered	down in the little car.
Alba crouched	when she saw the deep river.
The prowling	seemed as deep as the sea.
Alba's chest	wind got trapped in the cloth.

Teaching aims: This activity includes new vocabulary introduced in Book 10. It encourages the pupil to think about the meaning of the new words and to use them to construct a complete sentence.
Teaching guidelines: Cut the sentences into strips and cut along the centre line. Ask the pupil to match the two parts of the sentence so that they make sense. The pupil may need a reminder of what the words mean.

Book 10: Postcard home

Dear Mum,

First

Then

In the end

Love from Alba xxx

Teaching aims: Comprehension and free writing

Teaching guidelines: Encourage the pupil to write about what happened in Book 10. The sentence starters provide useful cues for breaking the story into sections. Useful words are provided at the bottom of the page. The teacher can decide whether or not to offer these.

Useful words: howled ground toy car crown drown

Book 10: Punctuation

Capital letters and full stops

REMINDER – A sentence **begins** with a capital letter and **ends** with a full stop.

a cold wind blew around it tossed litter about and made alba cold she found a scrap of cloth on the ground

alba was resting under a tree when she saw a toy car she got into the toy car and let the wind carry her across the ground to the river

the wind swept the bag off alba's back she jumped out of the car and landed in a patch of flowers she was clowning around in the flowers until she saw the deep river

Did you spot?

8 missing full stops

10 missing capital letters

Book 11: River Flight

Phonic focus: phoneme 'ie' **Spellings:** i, igh, y and i–e

Contents

Page

Book 11: Word–building 'ie' words

l	igh	t
l	*igh*	*t*

Teaching aims:

- learn the spelling alternatives <i>, <y> and <igh> for the sound 'ie'
- be able to segment and blend words with these three different spellings

Teaching guidelines:
Use a white board on which three lines have been drawn. Print a card from the appendix for the spellings <i>, <y> and <igh>. Add these to the cards with the letters of the alphabet from previous levels.

Teach word–building with the spellings <i>, <y> and <igh>:
Select a word from the lists below. Teachers can choose whether to start work with one spelling of the sound or whether to begin with multiple spellings. Use only the letters needed to build that word and jumble them up. Ask the pupil to build that word by listening to the sounds in the words and segmenting all the sounds in the words, one at a time. The pupil then brings down each card once he/she has segmented the sound in the word. Ask the pupil to read the word he/she has built. Ask the pupil to write the word under the lines, saying the sounds as he/she writes each sound. Draw more lines for longer words.

Word lists for word–building, reading and spelling:

i	y	igh
mind find rind	fly fry try	sigh light right
wild pint blind	spy sky dry	might bright
grind child	July reply deny	slight fright

Book 11: Word–building 'i–e' words

w		f			___ ___ ___ ___
t		m			___ ___ ___ ___
d		v			___ ___ ___ ___
n		n			___ ___ ___ ___
s	p		k		___ ___ ___ ___
g	l		d		___ ___ ___ ___

i	e	i	e	i	e	i	e	i	e	i	e

Teaching aims:

- learn the spelling <i–e>for the sound 'ie'
- be able to segment and blend words with this spelling

Teaching guidelines:

Cut out the 'ie' cards. Ask the pupil to cut along the central line in the spelling cards and insert the split spelling of the 'ie' in the words above. Ask the pupil to say the sounds as they blend them into a word.

Book 11: Timed reading 'i–e' words

Beat your own record!

pin	pine	fin	fine	dim	dime	pip	pipe
rip	ripe	kit	kite	shin	shine	Tim	time
Sid	side	rid	ride	slid	slide	grip	gripe
spin	spine	trip	tripe	still	stile	pill	pile

Teaching guidelines: Ask the pupil to read the text as fast as possible to try to beat his/her own time. You will need a timer for this activity.

Book 11: Reading and spelling 'ie' words with <igh> and <i–e> spellings

high	✓
sigh	
thigh	
slight	

bike	
wide	
spike	
stripe	

Teaching aims: Reading and spelling 'ie' words with the spellings <igh> and <i–e>.

Teaching guidelines: Fold this sheet along the dotted line. Ask the pupil to read the words on the left and tick the words she/he has read correctly. Ask the pupil to turn over the sheet and dictate the words to the pupil. Ask the pupil to spell the words by segmenting and sounding out the sounds as she/he writes them on the lines. Ask the pupil to open the sheet and tick the words she/he has spelled correctly.

Book 11: Reading and spelling 'ie' words with <i> and <y> spellings

kind	✓	_ _ _ _	
pint		_ _ _ _	
blind		_ _ _ _ _	
grind		_ _ _ _ _	

spy		_ _ _	
cry		_ _ _	
July		_ _ _ _	
shy		__ _	

Teaching aims: Reading and spelling 'ie' words with the spellings <i> and <y>.

Teaching guidelines: Fold this sheet along the dotted line. Ask the pupil to read the words on the left and tick the words she/he has read correctly. Ask the pupil to turn over the sheet and dictate the words to the pupil. Ask the pupil to spell the words by segmenting and sounding out the sounds as she/he writes them on the lines. Ask the pupil to open the sheet and tick the words she/he has spelled correctly.

Book 11: Reading and sorting words with 'ie' spellings

i	y	igh	i–e
fly	kind	bike	might
stripe	sky	white	blind
pint	spy	bright	slide
thigh	drive	guy	wild
July	light	find	five
mice	grind	mine	fry
high	dine	mind	dry
child	wide	try	slight

Teaching guidelines: Photocopy this page onto card and cut into reading cards. Read and sort the cards out according to the 'ie' spellings. The cards at the top of the sheet can be used as headings for each spelling. These spellings can be recorded on the following sheet.

Book 11: Spellings: 'ie'

i

i–e

y

igh

Teaching guidelines: List the words from the reading and sorting cards according to the spelling of the sound 'ie'.

Book 11: Reading and spelling

Two-syllable words with 'ie' spellings

Word	Read	Spelling	Spelled
light/ning	✓	_ ____ _ /_ _ ___	
dis/**li**k**e**		_ _ _ /_ _ _ _	
wr**i**/ting		___ _ /_ _ ___	
fl**y**/ing		_ _ _ /_ ___	
l**i**n**e**s/man		_ _ _ _ _ /_ _ _	
be/h**i**nd		__ /_ _ _ _	
t**y**/ping		__ /_ _ ___	
k**i**nd/ness		_ _ _ _ /_ _ ___	
day/l**igh**t		___ /_ ___ _	

Teaching aims: Reading and spelling words with alternative spellings of the sound 'ie'.

Teaching guidelines: Fold this sheet along the dotted line. Ask the pupil to read the words on the left and tick the words she/he has read correctly. Ask the pupil to turn over the sheet and dictate the words to the pupil. Ask the pupil to spell the words by segmenting and sounding out the sounds as she/he writes them on the lines. Ask the pupil to open the sheet and tick the words she/he has spelled correctly.

Book 11: Reading practice

Two-syllable words with 'ie' spellings

(Syllables split)

po lite	pipe line	lines man
night light	prize fight	coll ide
bright ness	blind fold	play time
life boat	fight er	bi ble
cry ing	de ny	de light
Fri day	gi ant	py thon
night dress	shy ly	Two-syllable words with 'ie' spellings (Alba Book 11)

Teaching aim: Reading practice

Teaching guidelines: Photocopy this page onto card and cut into reading cards.

Book 11: Reading practice

Two-syllable words with 'ie' spellings

polite	pipeline	linesman
nightlight	prizefight	collide
brightness	blindfold	playtime
lifeboat	fighter	bible
crying	deny	delight
Friday	giant	python
nightdress	shyly	Two-syllable words with 'ie' spellings (Alba Book 11)

Teaching aim: Reading practice

Teaching guidelines: Photocopy this page onto card and cut into reading cards.

Book 11: 4–in–a–row game 'ie'

child	dive	thigh	rind	Mike
dine	cry	high	mind	mine
sly	kind	bride	spy	wind
blind	wipe	dry	flight	why
knight	sigh	pint	white	slight
smile	July	right	sty	mild
hide	dive	thigh	rind	bike

A game for two players: Play with two sets of coloured counters. Players take turns to read a word and put a counter on it. The winner is the first to get four of his or her counters in a row in any direction. The winner places a counter on a bird. The game is played four times until all the birds are covered.

Book 11: Stepping stones reading game ‘ie’ words

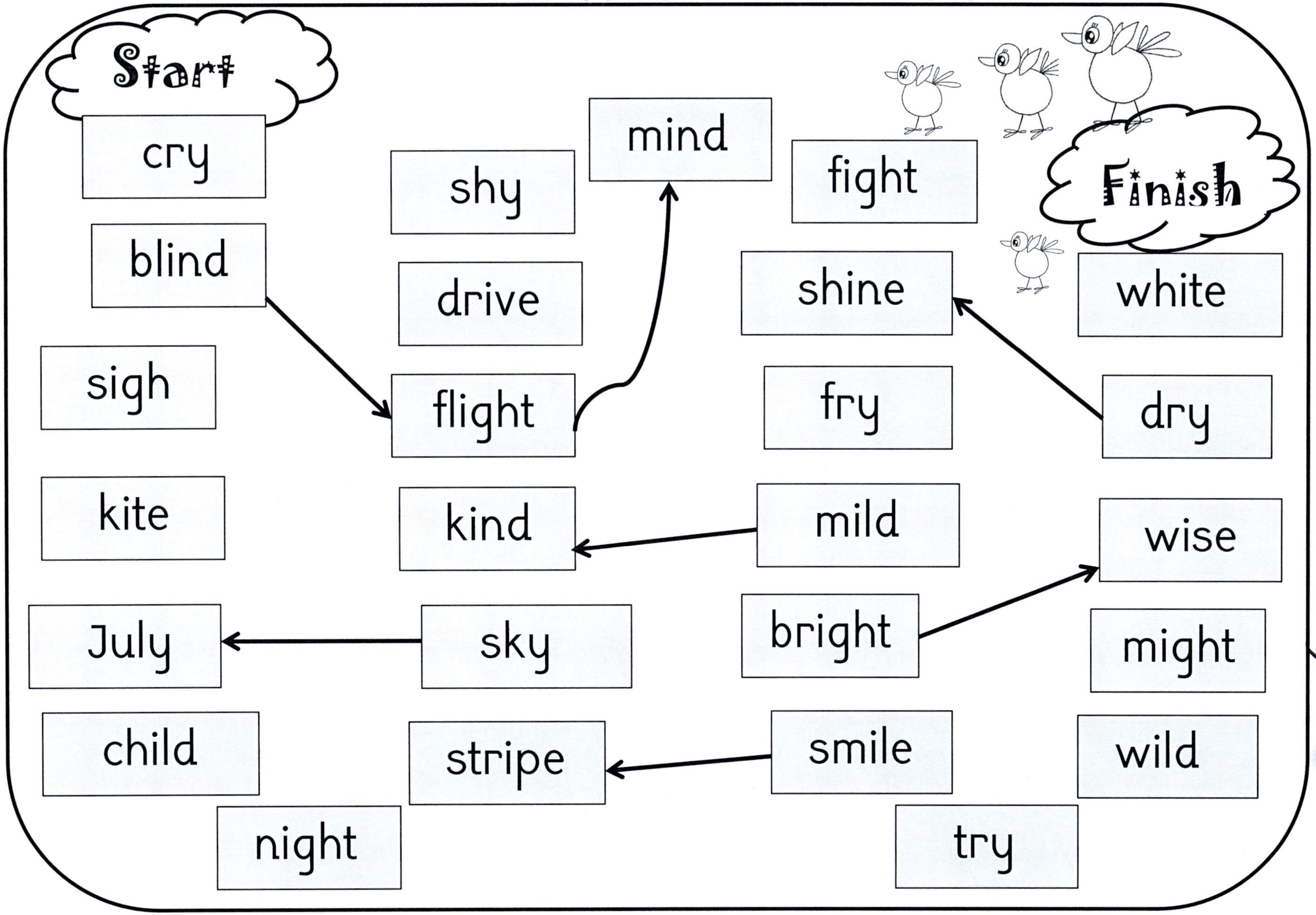

A game for 1–4 players: Play with counters and dice.
Players should read aloud the words that they land on at the end of each turn and follow the direction arrows if they land on them.

Book 11: Questions for discussion

Chapter 1

1. Why is Alba anxious that it is getting dark? (page 1)
2. What does she see on the riverbank that she hopes will help her? (page 3)

Chapter 2

1. What does Alba remember about magpies? (page 4)
2. Why does Alba's chest tighten when she sees Max? (page 6)

Chapter 3

1. How does Alba attract the magpie's attention? (page 7)
2. How do you think Alba feels to be so high up in the sky? (page 9)

Chapter 4

1. Why does the magpie cry out in surprise? (page 11)
2. Which three things is Alba happy about at the end of the story? (page 12)

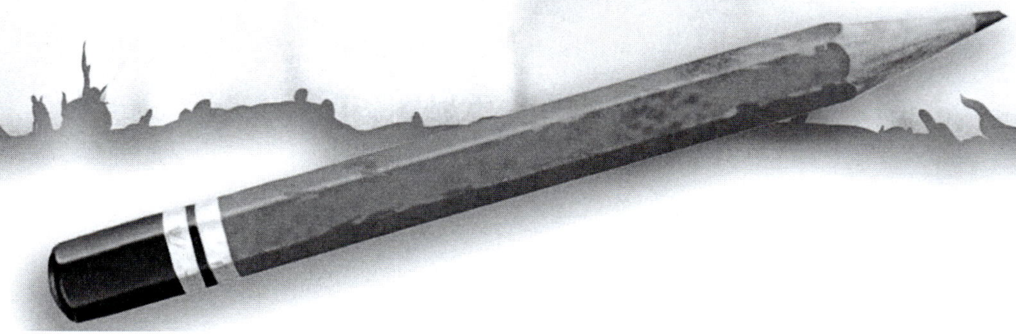

Teaching aims: Speaking and listening skills, comprehension and vocabulary.

Teaching guidelines: These questions can be discussed after reading the text

Book 11: True or false?

	yes	no
Alba was frightened of the wild animals.		
Alba saw a bright red bird on the riverbank.		
A sweet packet was lying in the mud.		
A cockroach was hiding inside the packet.		
The magpie grabbed the packet and took flight.		
Alba bit the magpie to make him drop her.		
The magpie dropped Alba in a pile of leaves.		
Alba decided to rest in the tree for the night.		

Teaching aim: Comprehension
Teaching guidelines: Ask the pupil to read the sentences and tick the boxes according to whether they are true or false.

Book 11: Picture the scene

The magpie is holding Alba inside a crisp packet.

The wild river is under them.

A plastic bottle is floating on the river.

The magpie is holding a leaf in his beak.

Teaching aims: Following instructions, comprehension and vocabulary

Teaching guidelines: Encourage the pupil to read the text carefully and draw the details of the picture as described in the text.

Book 11: Alba's diary

I had to cross the wild river. A magpie gave me a ride inside a crisp packet. I was glad to get away from Max. The magpie dropped me into a pine tree.

I _ _ _ to _ _ _ _ the

_ _ _ _ _ _ _ _. A

_ _ _ _ _ _ _ _ _ _ _ a

_ _ _ _ _ _ _ _ _ _ a

_ _ _ _ _ _ _ _ _ _. I was

_ _ _ _ to _ _ _ _ _ _

_ _ _ _ _ _ _.

The _ _ _ _ _ _ _ _ _ _

_ _ into a _ _ _ _ _ _ _.

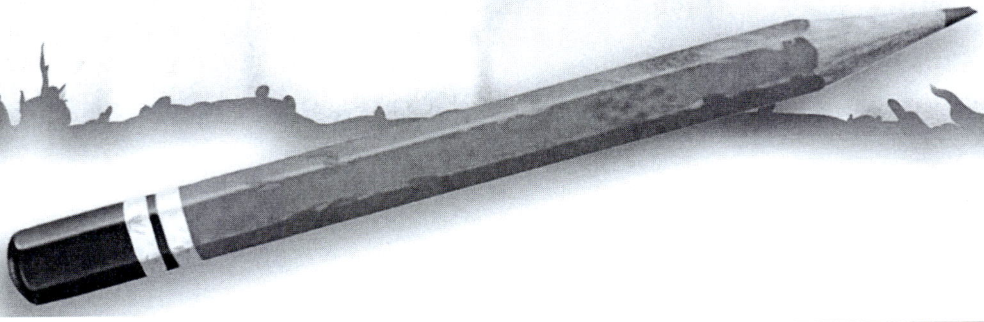

Teaching aims: Reading and spelling activity
Teaching guidelines: Encourage the pupil to copy the text at the top and insert it into the cloze exercise below it. Pupils should write a sound on each line e.g: h e l p. This activity can also be used for dictation.

Book 11: New words

New words in Book 11

lashed out – hit out at something
thigh – part of the leg between the hip and the knee
all of her might – with all of her strength
spiked – caught with a sharp spike

REMINDER – A sentence **begins** with a capital letter and **ends** with a full stop.

Alba lashed out	Alba's side.
Pine needles spiked	at the magpie.
Alba hit the magpie	all of her might.
Alba hit the bird with	on his thigh.

Teaching aims: This activity includes new vocabulary introduced in Book 11. It encourages the pupil to think about the meaning of the new words and to use them to construct a complete sentence.
Teaching guidelines: Cut the sentences into strips and cut along the centre line. Ask the pupil to match the two parts of the sentence so that they make sense. The pupil may need a reminder of what the words mean.

Book 11: Postcard home

Dear Mum,

First

Then

In the end

Love from Alba xxx

Teaching aims: Comprehension and free writing

Teaching guidelines: Encourage the pupil to write about what happened in Book 11. The sentence starters provide useful cues for breaking the story into sections. Useful words are provided at the bottom of the page. The teacher can decide whether or not to offer these.

useful words: night magpie flight might pine spike hide

Book 11: Punctuation

Capital letters and full stops

REMINDER – A sentence **begins** with a capital letter and **ends** with a full stop.

alba was next to the river she had to get across the wild water a magpie was pecking behind her

alba got inside a crisp packet the magpie snatched the packet and took flight into the sky alba had a ride across the wild river

when alba saw the other side of the river, she hit the magpie the magpie had such a surprise that he dropped alba she landed in a pine tree

Book 12: The Truth

Phonic focus: 'oo' **Spellings:** oo, u, u-e and ew

Contents

Book 12: Word-building 'oo' words

r	oo	m
r	*oo*	*m*

Teaching aims:

- learn the spelling alternatives <oo>, <ew> and <u> for the sound 'oo'
- be able to segment and blend words with these three different spellings

Teacher guidelines:

Use a white board on which three lines have been drawn. Print a card from the appendix for the spellings <oo>, <ew> and <u>. Add these to the cards with the letters of the alphabet from previous levels.

Teach word-building with the spellings <oo>, <ew> and <u>:

Select a word from the lists below. Teachers can choose whether to start work with one spelling of the sound or whether to begin with multiple spellings. Use only the letters needed to build that word and jumble them up. Ask the pupil to build that word by listening to the sounds in the words and segmenting all the sounds in the words, one at a time. The pupil then brings down each card once he/she has segmented the sound in the word. Ask the pupil to read the word he/she has built. Ask the pupil to write the word under the lines, saying the sounds as he/she writes each sound. Draw more lines for longer words.

Word lists for word-building, reading and spelling:

oo	ew	u
food mood moon	flew grew	judo truth super
room roof broom	crew blew drew	plural
bloom scoop tooth	brew chew threw	

Book 12: Reading and spelling 'oo' words with <oo> and <u> spellings

roof	✓	___ _____ ___	
food		___ _____ ___	
broom		___ ___ _____ ___	
tooth		___ _____ _____	

Ruth		___ ___ _____	
judo		___ ___ ___ ___	
rural		___ ___ ___ ___ ___	
super		___ ___ ___ _____	

Teaching aims: Reading and spelling 'oo' words with the spellings <oo> and <u>.

Teaching guidelines: Fold this sheet along the dotted line. Ask the pupil to read the words on the left and tick the words she/he has read correctly. Ask the pupil to turn over the sheet and dictate the words to the pupil. Ask the pupil to spell the words by segmenting and sounding out the sounds as she/he writes them on the lines. Ask the pupil to open the sheet and tick the words she/he has spelled correctly.

Book 12: Reading and spelling 'oo' words with <ew> and <u–e> spellings

flew	✓
chew	
threw	
screw	

___ ___ _____	
_____ _____	
_____ ___ _____	
___ ___ ___ _____	

lute	
rude	
rule	
flute	

___ ___ ___	
___ ___ ___ ___	
___ ___ ___ ___	
___ ___ ___ ___ ___	

Teaching aims: Reading and spelling 'oo' words with the spellings <ew> and <u–e>.

Teaching guidelines: Fold this sheet along the dotted line. Ask the pupil to read the words on the left and tick the words she/he has read correctly. Ask the pupil to turn over the sheet and dictate the words to the pupil. Ask the pupil to spell the words by segmenting and sounding out the sounds as she/he writes them on the lines. Ask the pupil to open the sheet and tick the words she/he has spelled correctly.

Book 12: Reading and sorting words with 'oo' spellings

oo	ew	u	u–e

super	food	grew	intrude
threw	room	Ruth	rude
Luke	judo	blew	goose
troops	chew	rural	June
truth	flute	fool	screw
crew	broom	include	lute
brute	brew	scoop	tooth
choose	prudent	exclude	flew

Teaching guidelines: Photocopy this page onto card and cut into reading cards. Read and sort the cards out according to the 'oo' spellings. The cards at the top of the sheet can be used as headings for each spelling. These spellings can be recorded on the following sheet.

Book 12: Spellings: 'oo'

ew	oo	u	u–e

Teaching guidelines: List the words from the reading and sorting cards according to the spelling of the sound 'oo'.

Book 12: Reading and spelling

Two-syllable words with 'oo' spellings

r**oo**f/top	✓	_ __ _ / _ _ _	
in/tr**ude**		_ _ / _ _ _ _	
cash/**ew**		_ _ __ / __	
j**ew**/el		_ __ / _ _	
ex/cl**ude**		_ _ / _ _ _ _	
mush/r**oo**m		_ _ __ / _ __ _	
j**u**/do		_ _ / _ _	
sham/p**oo**		__ _ _ / _ __	
fl**u**/ent		_ _ _ / _ _ _	

Teaching aims: Reading and spelling words with alternative spellings of the sound 'oo'.

Teaching guidelines: Fold this sheet along the dotted line. Ask the pupil to read the words on the left and tick the words she/he has read correctly. Ask the pupil to turn over the sheet and dictate the words to the pupil. Ask the pupil to spell the words by segmenting and sounding out the sounds as she/he writes them on the lines. Ask the pupil to open the sheet and tick the words she/he has spelled correctly.

Book 12: Reading practice

Two-syllable words with 'oo' spellings

(syllables split)

ball **oon**	b**oo**st er	br**ew** er
ch**ew** ing	d**oo**d ling	f**oo**l ish
r**u**th less	h**oo** ver	in tr**ude**
in cl**ude**	sn**oo** ker	ch**oo**s ing
J**ew** ish	tatt **oo**	j**u** do
m**oo**n light	Pl**u** to	rac **oon**
sch**oo**l girl	r**u** ler	Two-syllable words with 'oo' spellings (Alba Book 12)

Teaching aim: Reading practice

Teaching guidelines: Photocopy this page onto card and cut into reading cards.

Book 12: Reading practice

Two-syllable words with 'oo' spellings

balloon	booster	brewer
chewing	doodling	foolish
ruthless	hoover	intrude
include	snooker	choosing
Jewish	tattoo	judo
moonlight	Pluto	racoon
schoolgirl	ruler	Two-syllable words with 'oo' spellings (Alba Book 12)

Teaching aim: Reading practice

Teaching guidelines: Photocopy this page onto card and cut into reading cards.

Book 12: 4-in-a-row game 'oo'

chew	cool	noon	brute	loom
bloom	truth	June	flew	threw
flute	crew	spoon	plume	rule
root	Luke	rude	stool	roost
prune	proof	ooze	zoo	boost
food	Jew	fluke	moon	blew
Ruth	school	drew	roof	lute

A game for two players: Play with two sets of coloured counters. Players take turns to read a word and put a counter on it. The winner is the first to get four of his or her counters in a row in any direction. The winner places a counter on a heart. The game is played four times until all the hearts are covered.

Book 12: Stepping stones reading game ‘oo’ words

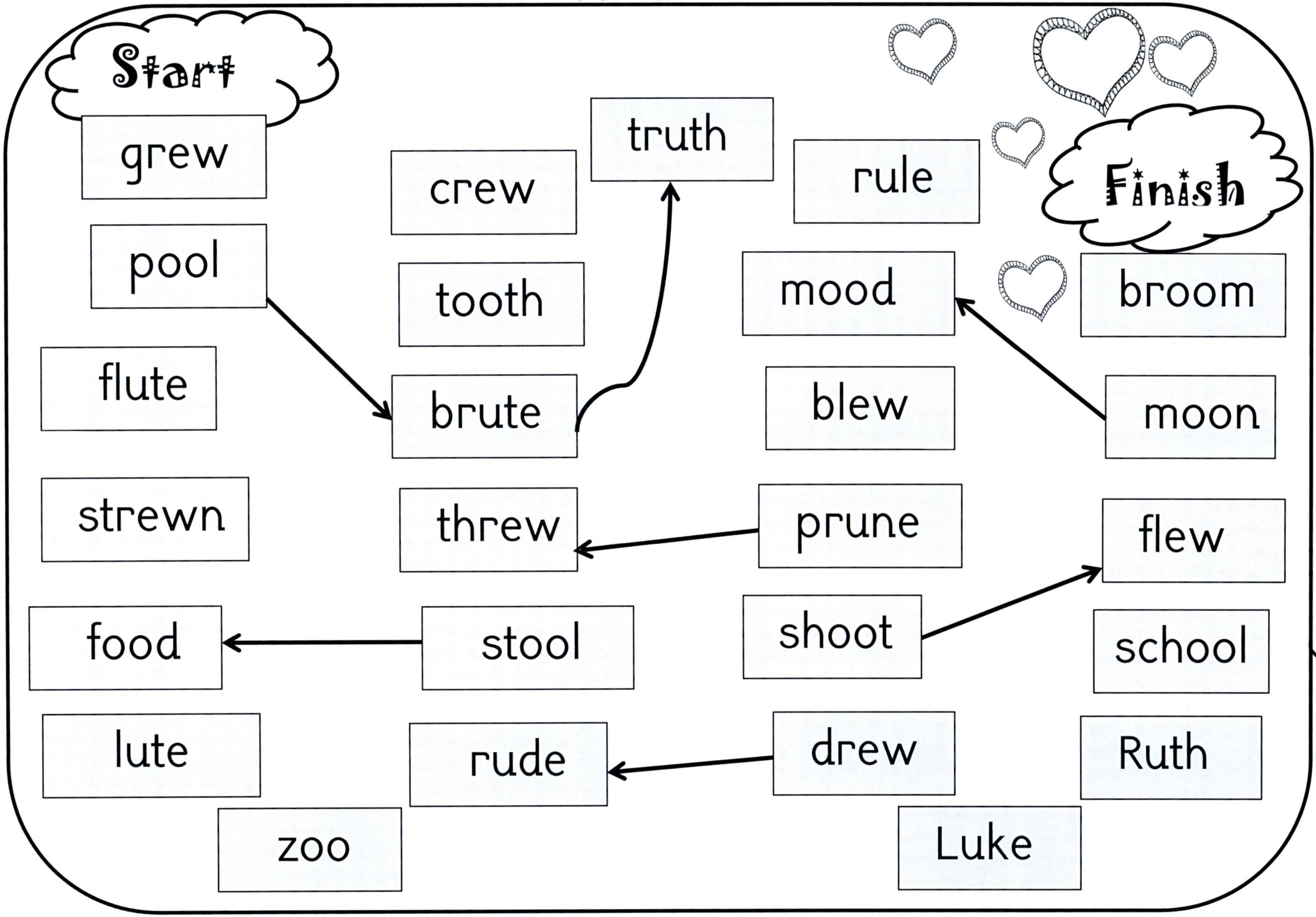

A game for 1–4 players: Play with counters and dice.
Players should read aloud the words that they land on at the end of each turn and follow the direction arrows if they land on them.

Book 12: Questions for discussion

Chapter 1

1. Why is Alba excited when she wakes up? (page 1)
2. What does she see that will help her get to Dad? (page 3)

Chapter 2

1. Why is this last apple pip so important? (page 6)

Chapter 3

1. What was the shrink ray invented to do? (page 7)
2. How can Dad help Alba? (page 8)
3 What is Alba first frightened of when she grows back to normal size? (page 10)

Chapter 4

1. How does Dad plan to stop Max? (page 11)
2. How do you think Alba feels now her adventure is over? (page 12)

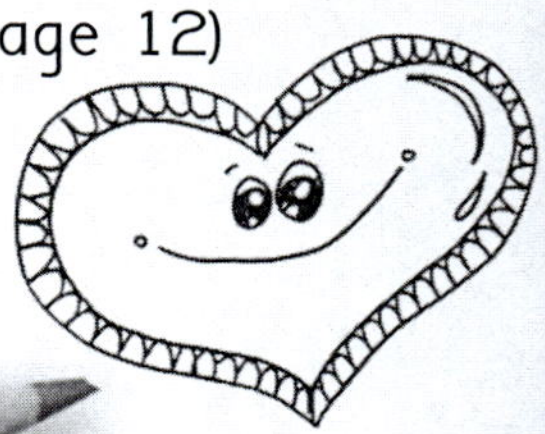

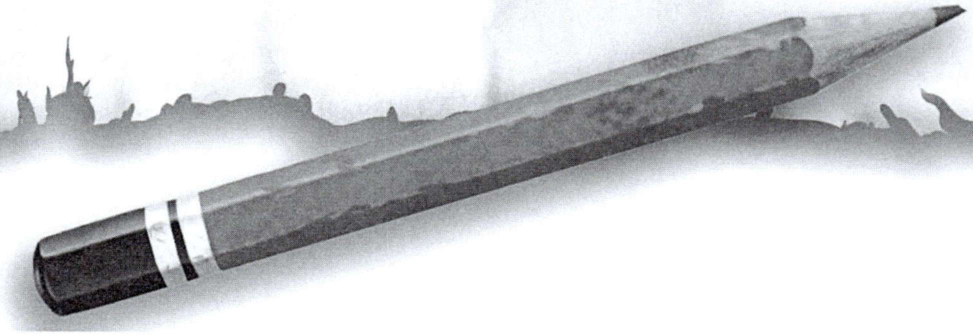

Teaching aims: Speaking and listening skills, comprehension and vocabulary.

Teaching guidelines: These questions can be discussed after reading the text.

Book 12: True or false?

Statement	yes	no
When Alba woke up, she found she was nearly at the flat.		
Alba's dad was sitting at his desk.		
Alba clambered up a bookcase to reach her dad.		
Dad gave Alba a drink to reverse the shrinking.		
Max was back at the lab.		
The last apple pip was as important as gold.		
Alba was so happy to be going back to school.		

Teaching aim: Comprehension
Teaching guidelines: Ask the pupil to read the sentences and tick the boxes according to whether they are true or false.

Book 12: Picture the scene

Dad is holding a long spoon.

There is a striped sweet on the spoon.

The sweet has sticky goo on top.

Six big drops of goo are dropping from the spoon.

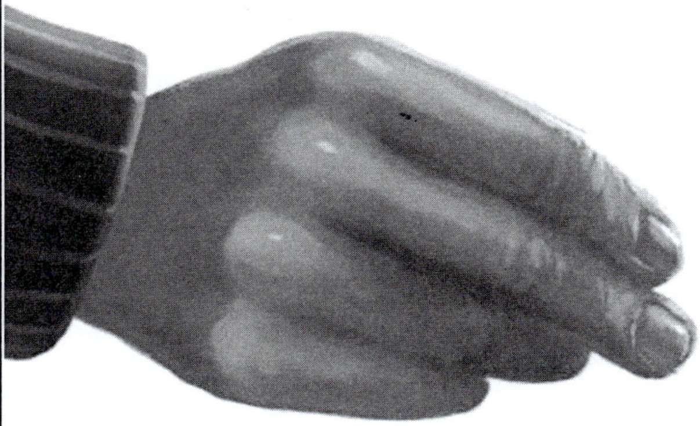

Teaching aims: Following instructions, comprehension and vocabulary

Teaching guidelines: Encourage the pupil to read the text carefully and draw the details of the picture as described in the text.

Book 12: Alba's diary

I woke up next to the lab! I went in and found Dad. Dad gave me a horrid sweet to make me grow! He sent his men to find Max. The apple pip is safe at last!

I _ _ _ _ _ _ _ _ _ _

to the _ _ _! I _ _ _ _

_ _ _ _ _ _ _ _ _ _ _ _.

_ _ _ _ _ _ _ _ _ a

_ _ _ _ _ _ _ _ _ to

_ _ _ _ _ _ _ _ _! _ _

_ _ _ _ his _ _ _ to

_ _ _ _ _ _ _. The _ _ _

_ _ _ is _ _ _ _ _ _

last!

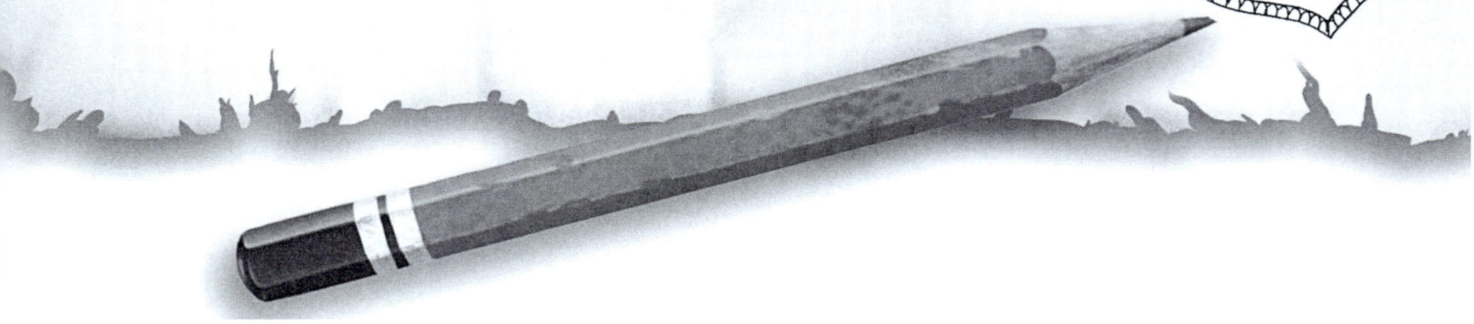

Teaching aims: Reading and spelling activity
Teaching guidelines: Encourage the pupil to copy the text at the top and insert it into the cloze exercise below it. Pupils should write a sound on each line e.g: h e l p. This activity can also be used for dictation.

Book 12: New words

New words in Book 12

roost – a place to rest or stay
gloomy – feeling hopeless
brooding – full of sad thoughts
drooping – bending or hanging down
clambered – climbed up using hands or feet
stooped – bent her head and shoulders down

REMINDER – A sentence **begins** with a capital letter and **ends** with a full stop.

The plant had	and feeling gloomy.
Alba clambered	so she would not hit the roof.
Dad was brooding about Alba	long, drooping leaves.
Alba was sitting	up the smooth stems of the plant.
Alba stooped	in her roost in the tree.

Teaching aims: This activity includes new vocabulary introduced in Book 12. It encourages the pupil to think about the meaning of the new words and to use them to construct a complete sentence.
Teaching guidelines: Cut the sentences into strips and cut along the centre line. Ask the pupil to match the two parts of the sentence so that they make sense. The pupil may need a reminder of what the words mean.

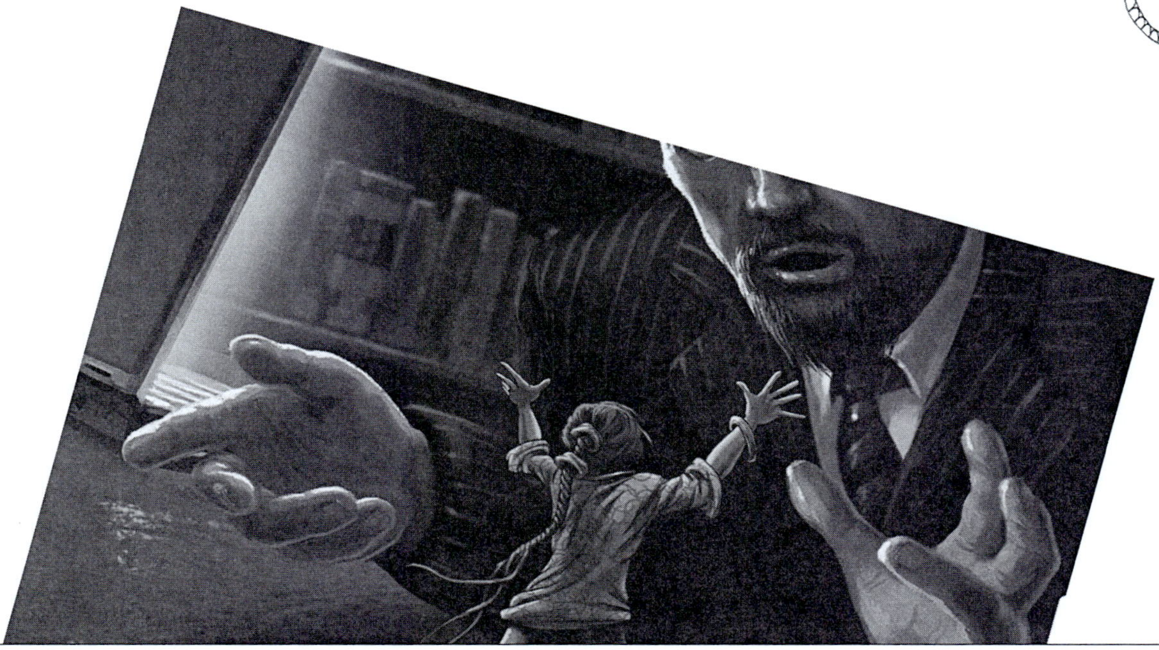

Dear Mum,

First

Then

In the end

Love from Alba xxx

Teaching aims: Comprehension and free writing

Teaching guidelines: Encourage the pupil to write about what happened in Book 12. The sentence starters provide useful cues for breaking the story into sections. Useful words are provided at the bottom of the page. The teacher can decide whether or not to offer these.

Useful words: roost scooped sweet zoomed school

Word-building cards

Alphabet

a	b	c	d
e	f	g	h
i	j	k	l
m	n	o	p
q	r	s	t

These cards can be photocopied onto card and used for word-building activities.

Alphabet continued

u	v	w	x
y	z		

Spellings for Book 4

sh	ch	tch	th

These cards can be photocopied onto card and used for word-building activities.

Word-building cards

Spellings for Book 5

ck	ng	qu	wh
le			

Spellings for Book 6

ay	ai	a

These cards can be photocopied onto card and used for word-building activities.

Word-building cards

Spellings for Book 7

ee	ea	y	ey
e			

Spellings for Book 8

o	ow	oa

Spellings for Book 9

er	ir	ur

These cards can be photocopied onto card and used for word-building activities.

Word–building cards

Spellings for Book 10

ow	ou

Spellings for Book 11

igh	y	i

Spellings for Book 12

oo	u	ew

These cards can be photocopied onto card and used for word-building activities.